Death & the Pagan

Philip Wright
&
Carrie West

Alphard

First published in Great Britain by ignotus press 2004
BCM-Writer, London WC1N 3XX
© Philip Wright & Carrie West 2004

British Library Cataloguing in Publication Data
ISBN: 1 903768 21 7

Printed in Great Britain by A2 Reprographics
Set in Baskerville Old Face 11pt

Cover photograph supplied by Natural Fencing

Contents

Chapter One

Perceptions of Death
Death & the Maiden (Schubert)

> *"Christianity has made of death a terror which was
> unknown to the gay calmness of the Pagan."*
> [Ouida: Marie Louise de la Ramée 1839-1908]

Here in the West, death is still generally looked upon as the last taboo - a fearful subject that must be avoided at all costs and, despite promises of 'everlasting life', much of this Western fear stems from Christian theological thinking, which still regards death as the penalty or punishment of sin. This colourful imagery, which is reflected in Dante's *Divine Comedy*, has fuelled the rhetoric of the evangelical factions ever since.

The great medieval and Victorian death-cults also kept a firm grip on the imagination of all classes of society, right up until the Great War of 1914-18. According to Kate Berridge, author of *Vigor Mortis*, "The annihilation of so many, the government policy of not repatriating the war dead for family burial ... caused a seismic shift in the emphasis put on different rituals. After the Great War the emphasis shifted from the body to the memory. At the same time, the demotion of the significance of the body in death rituals was accompanied by the promotion of rituals of remembrance." The First World War did indeed drastically alter the 'course of death rites' for the 21ˢᵗ century.

As *Vigor Mortis* goes on to explain. "It separated funerary ritual from commemoration, mourning from remembrance, private grief from public acts of remembering. This emphasis reverberates to the present day in low-key private cremations followed by large, more sociable memorial services."

Among the growing number of pagan cults, death is more than likely to be viewed as the next stepping-stone to a higher spiritual plane and rebirth, and for the more traditional of the revivalist groups, the 'presence' of the body remains an integral part of the funerary rites. For the vast majority of pagans, however, their perception of death is still greatly influenced by the fundamentals of socio-Christian thinking, insofar as Jesus may not want them for a sunbeam – but the 'Goddess' does. Pagans may not subscribe to the last trip to Heaven ... they winter in the Summerlands instead ... and in terms of ritual, most pagan funerary observances tend to be happy-clappy affairs, but retaining a subconscious overlay of gender-bender, eco-green Christianity.

Unfortunately, for non-pagans, the popular image of paganism is drawn from the annual debacle at Stonehenge, and the funeral industry's more personal encounters with those of grand titles, sporting robes made out of second-hand curtains and trying to appear important. With *this* image in mind, it is not difficult to understand why funeral staff fight shy of the possibility of having the local 'crem' turned into a circus. There is also the additional problem of the religious, or social persuasion, of the departed's nearest and dearest, many of whom many not even know what a Wiccan is, never mind attending the burial rites of one.

Regardless of the *personal* religious belief of the deceased, funerals are notorious for creating and furthering family feuding, and the last thing we need to cope with when saying goodbye to a dear friend, is a monumental punch-up between the family and the pagan contingent on the steps of the chapel of rest. As most pagans are fully aware, folk trend to lash out at things they don't understand and unless the family has been consulted, there may be some unpleasantness if the deceased's family are staunchly mainstream-religious.

Over My Dead Body!

A little forward planning can prevent the situation that happened to two members of our own Order, a married couple, who died within a very short space of time and in both cases, none of the pagan community were unable to pay their respects. Although they were both highly respected and well-known witches, the son was evangelical, and due to there being no instructions left as to the method of burial of *their* choosing, through sheer spite he took it into his head to have his parents buried according to Christian rite, even though he knew they were lifelong pagans. The father (who died first) was cremated but to this day, no one knows where his ashes lie; the mother was buried in a churchyard ... and all the friends they had made over the years were deliberately excluded from attending. All that marks their passing are two trees planted in their memory by the Woodland Trust and paid for by donations from the witches who needed to show them some kind of honour.

Unless specific instructions are left as to the type of funeral that is required, the arrangements will become the responsibility of the executors or the family, who will do what *they* feel is right. To avoid any sort of embarrassment or unpleasantness, all adult pagans should leave instructions in their Will detailing how they wish their remains to be disposed of, and this should be made known to the immediate family. If a Will has already been drawn up, then add a codicil to the document so that no one is left in any doubt as to what those wishes are.

Nevertheless, in *The Good Death Guide*, Michael Dunn raises a very important point. Did you know that although you can make your wishes known about your funeral, or the disposal of your body, "the curious thing is that you have no real say over what happens to this most personal of possessions: when you are dead your body is 'un-ownable' and you have no further rights in the matter of its disposal ... but do let your wishes be known before then. Lack of clarity can lead to some unfortunate results."

It is probably fair to say that the majority of pagans would prefer some form of 'natural' burial, and fortunately this is something that is also becoming more and more popular with mainstream Christianity. Even up to five years ago, natural burial would have been considered suspiciously 'alternative' but with the spate of celebrity funerals where they have opted for natural burial, the concept is now socially acceptable. Until recently, the form of burial was probably the biggest hurdle any pagan family had to overcome, but with the funeral industry now showing a more sympathetic approach, this is one less pressure removed from having to make decisions at a difficult time.

As with most other pagan 'rites of passage', however, there is no pre-prescribed format for a funeral. In *Life-Rites*, Aeron Medbh-Mara gives an example of the type of rites carried out by those in certain areas of traditional Craft, which can be performed privately by the coven or group, and publicly at the crematorium. Problems often arise, however, when the deceased belongs to one of the revivalist factions such as Norse, Druid, Egyptian or Celtic Traditions, where the rites demand a much more esoteric application. Again, generally speaking, none of these Traditions have recognised funerary rites that could be deemed suitable for public performance.

Come for your inheritance and you
may have to pay for the funeral
[Jewish proverb]

The truth of the matter is, that unless we are terminally ill, none of us know when we will die ... but it can happen at anytime and at any age, as a result of crime, accident, or undetected illness. The important thing is, that we discuss our wishes with our nearest and dearest. Not only should we discuss the method of our disposal, but also who will assume the responsibility for it. An increasing number of pagans have chosen a hand-fasting (i.e. pagan marriage) rather than a legally binding civil ceremony, and this could lead to all manner of difficulties in the event of an unexpected death.

As we have mentioned earlier in the chapter, a dead person has no rights, and so it is important to ensure that our partner is not left in the lurch, should we die intestate (i.e. without having made a Will). Most people assume that everything they own will pass to their partner after they die but automatic inheritance only applies:

> ➤ If we are married to our partner
> ➤ If there are no living children, parents or siblings
> ➤ If our property and estate does not exceed £233,000

As *The Good Death Guide* also points out: "Imagine you fell out with your parents thirty years ago and have since lived happily in an unmarried or a homosexual relationship – if you have not made a Will, your parents will get everything. Fairness and moral rights don't come into it; the law lays down strict rules to do with inheritance."

It's Good to Talk

By and large, pagans appear to have less fear in about *talking* about death but still very few actually make any definite arrangements. This may stem from the fact that they are not aware of the options open to them, rather than any reluctance to make a decision over what happens to their earthly remains.

"My grandmother always said that she wanted her ashes 'scattered to the four winds' and when the time came, the family complied with her wishes," remembers a friend. "Unfortunately, human ashes are like cat litter and 'scattering' doesn't work like that. The problem was solved when my mother tripped over a tree root and grandmother was literally deposited down a rabbit hole. I still smile to myself when I think of it, simply because my grandmother wouldn't have minded keeping company with the rabbits in the least."

And here are just a few of the comments made by members of our own coven:

"Just take me a long way out into the country and dump my ashes in the woods."

"I want to be buried in my robes, in a woodland setting."

"I want to be taken out to sea, and my ashes scattered on the waves."

"My family have had my instructions and my ashes, together with those of my dog, are going to be scattered on a specific mountainside in Wales."

"My ashes will go in my parent's grave in the village where I was born. Despite it being a Christian graveyard, I will feel as though I've come full circle."

"I want a woodland burial, and an oak tree planted on top."

Although everyone expressing his or her own individual wish here is a devout witch, there is nothing that cannot be arranged by via an ordinary funeral director. There is some comfort in knowing that the actual burial or disposal of the ashes now presents very little problem ... where the majority of pagans are poorly served is in the provision of the 'last rites' for the dying, and the content of the actual burial service.

If someone dies unexpectedly as a result of an accident, crime or sudden illness, the family may well go into shock and not be capable of making any informed or rational decision concerning funeral arrangements. On the other hand, where a friend or family member is suffering from a degenerative condition, the outcome is known but it may take months or years before death occurs. Even so, people put off talking about the funeral on the grounds that it seems like wishing them dead. As a result, when the end comes, suddenly or slowly, no one knows what to do, or to whom to turn for advice about the options available to them and the deceased may be subjected to a funeral that is entirely inappropriate for their beliefs.

"Death is not the greatest loss in life
The greatest loss is what dies inside us while we live."
[Norman Cousins]

Assisted Death

Although since the early 1960s it hasn't been a crime to take, or attempt to take your own life, it is an offence under the Suicide Act 1961 for someone to help you. As *The Good Death Guide* points out, however, that "in spite of the threat of prosecution, there is no doubt that we are generally in favour of assisted dying in certain circumstances ...there is less support for a more liberal law from religious groups, most of which have strong feelings about the sanctity of life, or the significance of a 'natural' death."

Richard Marriott, who comes from a pagan family and currently studying for a medical degree, submitted the following viewpoint:

"Before discussing the issues surrounding assisted death, or euthanasia, it is important to establish the true meaning and from where it is derived. Euthanasia comes from *eu* and *thanatos*, meaning quite literally 'gentle' or 'easy death'. It once referred to death in one's sleep, a peaceful way, without suffering. More recently it has become more associated with the painless killing of someone to end their suffering, or a 'mercy killing' as it is now recognised by the tabloids.

What is euthanasia?

Is it murder ... or an easy way to end someone's suffering at the hands of debilitating disease? Firstly, there are two kinds of euthanasia, and like a lot of things there are direct and indirect forms.

Direct is where someone is actively helped to die i.e. with drugs, which is illegal in the UK. Indirect is where someone is allowed to 'slip away' by means of being placed on intravenous fluids without feeding the body, which allows the person to die. This is only used when someone is proven unable to make any improvement, or when they or the next of kin, have requested for this to happen. The I.V. fluids provide comfort, but even without fluids a comatose patient can still survive for over a fortnight. Would you like to see someone you love stay like that for two long weeks?

The debate of whether euthanasia should be legalised, revolves around the decision of an individual to take their own life and their mental state at the time. Other factors include religious pressure and human rights. Recently, a couple travelled to Switzerland to take advantage of the country's pro-euthanasia law, but the debate wasn't about their actual death, it was the fact that *neither* of them had health problems and had made a decision to die together. This instance underlines in many sceptics' eyes the problems that could arise from taking decisions due to the fear of what *could* be around the corner, and the possibility of people throwing away their lives for no valid reason.

The price of keeping a critically ill patient alive, even when there is no chance of recovery, is a costly affair and most nursing staff would agree to euthanasia if it was the *individual's* decision, and not due to peer pressure from the family. The patient concerned would need to make a formal decision in advance, and most likely under-go some sort of psychological test to determine their state of mind at the time of the decision.

Hospitals have an average of around 70% elderly in care; a small number of these will probably never see the outside world again, and some believe that if a decision on releasing the individual from their suffering could be made, then it might help them to find peace. A staff nurse said: "People *should* be allowed to decide how they're going to die, rather than suffer and die a less dignified way." Needless to say, this would require a clear statement of intent from the *patient*, or relatives could start justifying their own actions by saying: "It's what she would have wanted," even though it wasn't!

At the moment, it is possible to waver the right to receive intravenous fluids but this decision can still be overturned by family, or by a doctor. Another issue is the waving of rights to be resuscitated, which starts to open the door to euthanasia. A deputy sister's view as that: "If someone does not want resuscitating, then as long as it's documented on a regular basis, that person will not be brought back to life, even if there is a high probability they would not suffer any health problems". This is course of action is more concerned with situations such as road accidents, and the person involved having some sort of documentation with them at all times, though it would be quite insensitive to attempt to confirm someone's wishes while they were actually dying.

The moral and human rights are used for both sides of the argument, but are usually associated with the pro-euthanasia stance of it being someone's final act of will or last request.

Does anyone actually have the right to tell us *how* to die, or dictate how long the dying process will last? This is one of the many reasons why a large number agree with euthanasia, including an auxiliary nurse, who thought that: "Euthanasia would give us as human beings the opportunity to decide our own fate, rather than having to suffer at the hands of some terrible conditions." Working in a care environment had shown her at first hand, the suffering that, particularly the elderly, have to go through. "When someone actually *wants* to be released you can understand why they want it to end; but when someone can only cry and scream in pain, the suffering is in the voice. Having to rely on others is something nobody likes, so the total dependency on carers must be a terrible ordeal for those of an independent mind."

Religion, however, is one thing that hardly ever changes: some follow their religion very strictly and others don't, but in a large number of cases it is the question of death that divides. The Catholic Church doesn't agree with euthanasia, on the grounds *you* are changing the destiny that was planned by God. "We should die when we are meant to, even if it means having to suffer or it will be seen as taking a short cut to God," was the view of another staff nurse. This actually means people should be willing to suffer for what they believe in, and in some cases, where for example, a child is too young to make any decision for themselves, they must do as the parents' decide.

Another concern for many is the idea that unscrupulous relatives, friends or even doctors, could influence the use of euthanasia, in order to receive money. The view of a staff nurse was that: "My main doubt would be the responsibility of others in the decision of one person's wish to die". The additional fear is that legal euthanasia could open the doorways for people to commit murder in order to turn a profit; which is why the any legally endorsed system would need continuous checks to make sure people were taking these important decisions for the right reasons and without coercion.

Perhaps one of the hardest things to face in life, is to watch someone slip away who you care about. For nursing staff, even strangers slowly dying isn't very pleasant to watch, so imagine being able to end all that suffering and waiting, by letting them go while they have their loved ones around them. A doctor commented: "If it was someone close then yes, it would be a good idea, but if it was a stranger you were dealing with then I'm not sure. As a doctor, I know its illegal, but if it was legalised then it would require very strict guidelines". Possibly here we come to the real crux of the matter. Something that we do, or decide for ourselves, is easy but something that shifts the responsibility onto others is where doubt creeps into the equation.

Death is an inevitability it happens to us all, some sooner, some later. When the time comes, most people would always prefer the choice of an easy passing to that of a lingering death. As individuals we all have the right to speak our mind but not pick our own fate.

The Voice From The Grave

So, if you and your family (or group members) have very definite ideas about what you want in terms of funerary rites and burial, then it is essential that you find out what the possibilities are and leave detailed instructions about your wishes. If these can be agreed in advance, it can save a lot of time and trouble for those appointed to carry out your wishes. For example:

- Where do you want to be buried/cremated.
- Is it necessary to buy a burial plot together?
- Are you to be buried in your robes?
- What type of funeral service do you want? (i.e. fully pagan or taking non-pagan members of the family into account.
- Who should officiate?
- Arc there any contact details for pagan organisations that can help?
- What should happen to your ashes?

- ✿ Are there any particular people who should be invited/excluded?
- ✿ Should there be some form of memorial/celebratory rites carried out after the funeral?
- ✿ Who should act as executor and take care of any magical personal effects?
- ✿ Are there any other requests?

These are all things we need to discuss with the family or group members, and make sure that those appointed executors of our Will have a good chance of outliving us! Other than that, we draw up a list of our wishes and lodge the document, together with our Will in the hands of a solicitor. If you have managed to give details of a pagan organisation that can advise on the spiritual/religious matters, then the solicitor can hand the instructions to the appointed funeral director. Those belonging to one of the established Traditions will have a better chance of getting what they want, as the priesthood will be in a position to explain the religious connotations of the deceased's request and the variances between the different pagan beliefs.

We are not, however, concerned here with the differentials that divide the pagan community but on convincing funeral directors, crematoria staff, health and care workers (as well as other pagans) that there *is* a very real need to cater for alternative beliefs at both the pre- and post-death stages. This need will become even more noticeable within the next few years as even more of those pagan trailblazers from the 1960s and 70s fall into the hands of care workers, nursing staff and ultimately, the death squad.

Chapter Two

Religious Belief
Inner Light (Harvey)

> *"I warmed both hands before the fire of life;*
> *It sinks and I am ready to depart."*
> [Walter Savage Landor 1775-1864]

Over half of the population believe in immortality in the spiritual sense and, almost without exception, some form of re-incarnation plays an intrinsic role in pagan belief. Although a large number of Christians also share this idea of a spiritual rebirth, the overall concept of paganism as a religion is often met with a high degree of scepticism and mistrust.

As Pascal Boyer observed in *Religion Explained*, when asked 'What is your religion?', many people will readily answer that they have *a* particular religion, indeed they *belong* to a religion with a particular *doctrine*. "People identify themselves as Jains, or Protestants, or Buddhists, and can usually describe the differences as a matter of doctrinal assumptions, of holding for instance that dead people can come back and show us the true path of salvation, that a unique god is watching our every action, that it is abhorrent to destroy any living thing, however humble, that the gods can protect you against illness or misfortune ..."

Being classed as pagan doesn't necessarily mean that an individual is following *a* religion with a particular doctrine; neither does it mean that pagans participate in common rituals that serve to strengthen a common identity. Again Pascal Boyer explains: "We must not mistake official norms for actual fact. This connection between having the same gods or the same practices, and being a community, may be more a statement of what *should* happen than a description of what does happen."

Because there is no real common denominator within pagan beliefs, care workers in general, and hospice staff in particular, have little practical information on which to act. Some may be genuinely alarmed by the sight of a pentagram, which for a good many, will suggest the wearer belongs to the 'Dennis Wheatley school of occultism'. There are, of course, other elderly patients to take into consideration, who may also become concerned by any overt displays of witchery and paganism.

This does not, for one moment, suggest that anyone should be forced to compromise their own particular religious beliefs, but a discreet word prior to admittance could nip any avoidable misunderstandings in the bud. Like the case of the elderly witch who was forced to go into a care home where the staff were constantly pushing his pagan symbols and magazines into drawers. He countered by asking a friend to bring him a black sweatshirt with 'Hail Satan' blazoned across the front in blood red. Over the weeks the situation deteriorated until one afternoon he discovered that all his pagan belongings and books had been removed from his room and a large brass crucifix placed on the bedside table. It made a *very* large hole in the window pane!

Whereas we would not justify this type of reaction by either party, it is nonetheless unreasonable to force anyone to suppress an expression of their own faith, when others can openly sport the trappings of a mainstream religion without let or hindrance. When people are approaching the end of their life, either through age or terminal illness, their faith is often the one thing that sustains them through the long hours of the night.

As we have seen in Chapter One, when it comes to the actual death and funerary rites, there was even less information available for funeral staff until 'The Pagan Perspective' by Suzanne Ruthven, was published by *The Funeral Service Journal* [2001], which went a long way in explaining some of the differences, and was favourably received by the publishers:

"It is generally accepted that there should be some kind of observance to mark the occasion of a person's death. Most people would also accept that everyone has the right to be buried or cremated according to the tenets of their own particular belief or faith. For those of pagan belief, the choices have been extremely limited despite the resurgence of 'official' pagan funeral rites in crematoria and, in more recent years, woodland burials.

In those early days, to mark a friend's passing, fellow pagans recited prayers and poetry since there was very little in the way of any suitable, publicly available funerary rites to which they could refer. More often than not, it was all a bit of a shambles, or an officiant from the British Humanist Association was called in but today, the pagan community has its own organisations that provide celebrants to mark these rites of passage according to the beliefs or wishes of the deceased.

Funeral directors, councils, crematoria and cemeteries are becoming increasingly aware of the growing need for pagan facilities but few realise that there are as many facets to paganism as there are in other religious communities. On one side there is what is more commonly referred to as 'broad-based paganism' – a nature-based spirituality that sees death as part of the natural life-cycle with karmic overtones. On the other, there are the formal revivalist traditions, such as the Celtic, Norse, Druid and Egyptian, whose funeral rites are more concerned with the transition of the soul.

The latter have more in common with the type of service found in the 1662 Prayer Book than with more modern forms of funerary rite, which now tend to be geared more casually towards family and friends saying goodbye to the departed. For the traditionalists, the funeral marks the beginning of the hazardous journey of the soul. There are certain propitiatory rites that need to be carried out on behalf of the deceased that can only be performed by an Initiate and member of the priesthood of that particular Tradition.

Normally with the best intentions, family and friends want to arrange a funeral the way the deceased would have wanted it and in accordance with their pagan beliefs. If, however, neither the family nor the funeral director have little idea of what those pagan beliefs entail, the resulting ceremony could give rise to embarrassment or, even worse, be offensive to many of those attending. At the same time, bringing in a complete stranger to conduct the ceremony can result in an impersonal and often irrelevant monologue that offers neither comfort for the mourners, nor guidance for the soul.

How often have we all heard the comments as we've left a funeral service: "I don't know who s/he was talking about, but it wasn't who's in the box!" or "John never believe in any of *that*." There is also the problem of images specific to one set of religious beliefs not intruding on the next. Over the years, there have been numerous complaints that pagan mourners have had to sit through a ceremony presided over by a crucifix. In reality, very few pagans are anti-Christian, but funeral staff would not subject Methodist, Hindu or Muslim mourners to praying under the symbol from a different faith and so why should pagans be expected to acquiesce. With such cavalier treatment – even just for the brief duration of the funeral service – is it any wonder that a feeling of bitterness can last long after the period of mourning has passed.

This is why there is a growing need for funeral staff to be aware of services provided by such independent organisations such as Green Undertakings, LifeRites and Traditional Life-rites Celebrants. All are linked to a network of celebrants who can advise on pagan funerary procedures and, where necessary, conduct the funeral service at a crematorium or woodland burial site.

Green Undertakings is an independent service operating in the Midlands and they specialise in eco-friendly funerals. As a spokesman for the company explained: "There are very few limitations to creating a meaningful personal ceremony and we can give unbiased advice on creating a ceremony befitting the individuality of the deceased."

The aim of LifeRites is to serve the needs of those individuals who hold no formal religious beliefs, or subscribe to nature-based spiritualities. Michael Murphy, a spokesman for Life-Rites, described his work as a celebrant in terms of "assisting the bereaved family or, in the case of the deceased having made a pre-funeral plan, to compose and carry out the funeral rite in accordance with those wishes, in a caring and sensitive manner."

By contrast, the role of Traditional Life-rites Celebrants (TLC) is to provide rites of passage for those who belong to established revivalist Traditions. According to Aeron Medbh-Mara, author of *Life-rites* and founder of TLC: "For us, the funeral service focuses totally on ensuring that the soul of the deceased is recognised and welcomed by their appropriate god(s) ands the rituals ensure that the soul passes through the correct 'landmarks' on this journey. During life we have every opportunity to make peace with our loved ones; the funeral rite is where we play the supporting role to enable them to reach the stars, or enter the Halls of Welcome. It is the deceased's moment of glory and the priest merely their guide."

['The Pagan Perspective' by Suzanne Ruthven, *The Funeral Service Journal* [2001]

This extract displays some of the differences in attitude between modern paganism, and those with a more formal history and as Pascal Boyer observes: "All religions, or so it seems, have something to say about death. People die but their shadows stay around. Or they die and wait for the Last Judgement. Or they come back in another shape. The connection between notions of supernatural agents and representations about death may take different forms in different human groups, but there is always some connection. Why is that so? One straightforward answer is that our concepts and emotions about death are quite simply the origin of religious concept. Mortality, it would seem, naturally produces questions that religion answers, and emotions that it helps alleviate."

Neo-paganism and Wicca are, in fact, still in their embryonic stages in religious terms, and far from having its focus on death, theirs' is a celebration of life. Wicca is the only religion that Britain has ever given to the world; with its foundations in the witchcraft revival championed by Gerald Gardner in the 1950s, it has become the fastest growing belief in the West. But despite the thousands who every year turn to paganism, there is still no unifying creed, nor any pagan 'Book of Common Prayer'. It is only now, when older pagans are getting ready to embark on their last great journey, that they are finding their needs are not being sympathetically catered for by the establishment.

Although it would be unfair to describe the revivalist Traditions as 'death-cults', much of their ritual *is* concerned with death – but in a more sublimated form. Those following the Paths of the old British, Norse, Celtic or Egyptian beliefs will, more likely than not, have been initiated into what is referred to as 'the Mysteries', a form of voluntarily simulated near-death-experience. Because of this ritual preparation, members of these revivalist Traditions are more likely to be able to call upon the help of fellow Initiates to help them 'cross over'. All this is not half as wacky as it may first sound: remember that the degree system within contemporary Freemasonry is still based on these very same ancient rites.

The problems that many dying pagans face, is not in finding a sympathetic burial squad, but in the acceptance and/or rejection by care staff. The fact also has to be faced that care or social workers still make uneasy bedfellows, since many older pagans retain vivid memories of the anti-occult campaigns of the 1960s and 1990s, which were instigated by members of these 'caring' professions. Those pagans who lived in fear and trembling of their children and grandchildren being dragged screaming from their beds at two o' clock in the morning, are the ones who now face the prospect of placing themselves in the hands of the very same caring professions that chose to believe the scaremongers.

In 1989, a publicity-seeking MP, unleashed a string of accusations in the House of Commons, claiming he had irrefutable proof that witches and pagans were molesting and murdering children in their 'satanic' rituals. From 1989 until 1994, hundreds of children were taken into care following night-raids on their homes, simply because local teachers, care workers and religious leaders made accusations against the parents on the flimsiest of 'evidence'. With

the benefit of hindsight, it seems incredible that a story with no sub-
stance could embroil nearly every level of Government, the police,
the NSPCC ... and then evaporate into thin air without a word of
apology or explanation to the pagan community.

Ignorance and religious intolerance still prefer to believe that
the wearing of a pentagram is tantamount to publicly admitting to
being a satanic devil-worshipper, so let's look at a couple of 'facts':

+ FACT: Satan plays no part in pagan belief, this is a wholly
  Christian concept.

+ FACT: Pagans don't worship what they don't believe in.

+ FACT: Only disenfranchised Christians worship Satan

Despite Professor Jean La Fontaine's Government-commissioned
report that laid the blame fairly and squarely on the doorsteps of
over-zealous social workers and vindictive evangelical fundamental-
ists, prejudice against pagan belief is still widespread.

*"For him who has faith, death, so far as it is his own death, ceases
to possess any quality of terror. The experiment will be over, the
rinsed beaker returned to the shelf, the crystals gone dissolving
down the waste-pipe; the duster sweeps the bench."*
[H. G.Wells, 1866-1946]

Cultural differences

Many of those following the revivalist Traditions, such as the Norse,
Druid, Egyptian or Celtic Paths will give a greater significance to a
fellow pagan's death.   These ancient cultures had established and
highly complex death rituals, which are more lengthy and elaborate
than we are generally used to seeing.   In these cultures, the process
of dying, preparing and disposing of the body, mourning and bereavement were linked to very specific practices: the Otherworld

journeying and the rebirth, or reincarnation, of the deceased.

It is therefore important to stress that any of these revivalist groups would strongly object to being lumped together under the general banner of 'paganism' when it is the matter of death, which so sharply divides them from the rest of the pagan community. It may be difficult for family, care workers and funerary staff to appreciate just how dissimilar the beliefs of the revivalist groups are from the less formal approach of contemporary Wicca and paganism, but the divisions *are* there and they are extremely important to those who follow that particular Path.

Let's go back to Pascal Boyer, who wrote: "This way of understanding religious ritual helps us understand, not just why gods are associated with rituals at all, but also what precise roles they are supposed to play in these occasions."

For the general pagan funeral, as in a Christian service, most are content to 'commend the soul' of the departed to their god: very few actually believe that deity to be present. In this case, the 'officiant' can be a member of the family, or a close friend – or a pagan priest may be brought in to do the job, even though they are not from the deceased own Path or Tradition, and may not have been known to the person whose funeral they are conducting. For most pagans, theirs' is a benign, benevolent deity who will shortly welcome the deceased into the Summerlands.

For the Traditionalists, however, things are much more hazardous and most believe that only an Initiate from their own faith can invoke deity. The Priest-Initiate would, hopefully, have helped them to 'cross over' and prepared them for the close encounter of an entirely different kind. For this is the realm of a harsher, more judgemental Being, who is more concerned as to whether the deceased has kept to the oath demanded and given upon Initiation. In some beliefs, lesser Beings can be summoned to act as a guide, and it is the Priest-Initiate's role to ensure that an appropriate entity is riding shotgun on that final journey. To bring in an outsider to perform such a task would be deemed tantamount to asking the milkman to officiate just because he happens to have pagan sympathies.

"I feel nothing, apart from a certain difficulty
in continuing to exist."
[Bernard de Fontenelle]

The Near-Death Experience

Within most of the genuine Mystery Traditions, death is viewed as a process of rebirth but the near-death experience is not confined to those of pagan belief. In *Exploring Spirituality*, the authors examined the subject, which crosses a wide range of cultures and religions, and appears to be markedly consistent in the reports. Being members of the pagan priesthood, they also had another perspective to offer ...

"The nearest thing to 'proof' [of life after death] are the consistent medical reports of the 'near death experiences' which often occur during or after surgery. These reports are nearly always identical in that patient floats through a long tunnel towards a brilliant light. Sometimes a figure appears to bar their entry, returning them to their earthly body and they survive to tell the tale. The figure is variously described as Jesus, an angel, or a deceased member of the family. These near death experiences give a tremendous amount of comfort to the recipient – but there is another side to consider.

There have also been numerous reports of near death experiences that take the patient down into darkness, or some other fearful realm, but these are infrequently mentioned publicly for fear of causing alarm. Imagine sinking into the abyss, falling into bottomless darkness and then being revived ... death would still hold all the terrors and none of the comforts for that recipient, who would assume that they were headed straight for hell. Others report seeing flames (rather than light), or experiencing a floating sensation as though suspended in a dark, watery environment.

On a spiritual level we can dispense with the equation of light = good; darkness = evil, because these are arbitrary concepts, not spiritual ones. Anyone who has even a passing interest in astrology will be familiar with the elemental groupings of earth, air, fire and water, that in esoteric terms align with the four cardinal points of the compass. The 12 signs of the zodiac also fall into Earth signs (Taurus, Virgo, Capricorn); Air signs (Gemini, Libra, Aquarius); Fire signs (Aries, Leo, Sagittarius) and Water signs (Cancer, Scorpio, Pisces), all of which are supposed to govern the way we think and react according to when and where we were born.

This belief that the stars and planets – or cosmic influences – rule our lives is a very ancient one dating back to the priesthoods of Chaldea and Babylon. Like all the archaic sciences, however, it became trivialised as the ancient wisdom was submerged under modernisation These grains of information were recorded for posterity but not the interpretation or understanding. If humans are made up of these basic elements then perhaps *that* is what we return to at death, before we re-emerge in another incarnation. Those whose element is Air *will* be drawn to the light, while those of elemental Earth will be drawn back into the bosom of Mother Earth. Elemental Fire doesn't represent the flames of hell, but cosmic fire, while elemental Water suggests the primordial waters from which everything originated.

This is only another theory, of course, but it does explain some of those awkward questions that always crop up when we're thinking about life, death and the Universe. If you think this is all nonsense, however, reflect on the fact that when the ancient astrologers claimed that people's lives were ruled by the stars, they were right in essence if not in detail. In *The Magic Furnace*, Marcus Chown demonstrated that 20th century scientific discovery has proven that we are far more intimately connected to events in the cosmos than anyone ever dared imagine, simply because those atoms that we carry around in our bodies originated in deep space!

These atoms were thrown out into space by the collapse of a giant star, adding to the swirling mass of gas and dust from which new stars were created. In the cooling process the heavy elements in the dust cloud became incorporated into our solar system. In turn these elements became part of the Earth and ultimately the first primitive living cells ... which means that 'every one of us was quite literally made in heaven. Each and every one of us is stardust made flesh' and scientific discovery compounds the mystical realisation of eternity ..."

[*Exploring Spirituality,* Suzanne Ruthven & Aeron Medbh-Mara – How-To Books]

All these issues amount to a hefty responsibility for those who are members of the pagan priesthood, but it is equally important to be able to explain to 'outsiders', i.e. funeral staff and care workers, *why* the different systems draw inferences from different cues, and often produce dissimilar expectations about the various aspects of a deceased's religion or beliefs. Very few people under thirty years of age would be able to cope well with all the responsibilities involved, yet many are all too hasty to accept the rank and titles which indicate that they *should* be able to deal with these matters, but all too often are lacking in practical experience.

So, choose your officiant wisely and remember that this is not a rehearsal: someone's soul may be put at risk.

Chapter Three

Death Watch
Night Ride & Sunrise (Sibelius)

"Death never takes the wise man by surprise;
he is always ready to go."
[Jean de la Fontaine 1621-1695]

As with all things in life, there comes a time when Death throws us a curved ball and we may find ourselves in the position of having to perform, or request someone to perform, funerary rites within a hospital environment, at the scene of an accident, or even in a stranger's home.   Over the years, within a pagan group or coven there will probably be relatively few deaths to content with, but there will come a time when we do have to perform services for our own members, or for those who may not be part of our immediate circle.   Those eventualities must be prepared for, and the wise member of the pagan priesthood is the one who prepares a 'mini rit-kit' containing a miniature collection of objects pertinent to our own Path or Tradition.

In all honesty, the majority of pagans lack the necessary knowledge, skills and experience to cope with a 'death watch' but if the person who is dying needs and requests the comfort of a member of the priesthood from his or her own Tradition, then they have every right to expect this to be provided.   Unfortunately, as Fiona Walker-Craven reported in *High Rise Witch* (aimed at housebound and disabled pagans), social and care workers often still consider those of pagan persuasion as being feeble-minded, and are more than likely to dismiss the more Traditional elements of belief as a sign of mental illness!

Up until the last century, most people died at home, but with more and more need for residential and hospice care, there will be an increased demand for places for elderly or terminally ill pagans, since it is estimated that one in five of us will eventually need full-time residential care. The founding of the hospice movement has gone a long way to improve the 'quality of life' for the dying and offers not only medical care but pays attention to the physiological, emotional, spiritual and family needs of the patients. Although many hospices have a religious foundation, patients and staff are not selected because they belong to a particular faith; they attempt to meet the needs of people from all cultures and religions – and those with no belief at all. Unfortunately, the supply by far outweighs the demand and nationally there are few beds available, even though the average life-expectancy for a hospice patient is six months or less.

In an ideal world, we would like to think that all those in the twilight of their life could reasonably expect to be looked after by staff sympathetic to their beliefs, but this is rarely the case. *The Good Death Guide* made the observation that within the social work profession "there is an emphasis on quality of life for residents but less attention to quality of dying. Staff are poorly trained and often kept too busy to sit with a dying person. So often a death is met with embarrassment and secrecy ..."

Some would say that perhaps this is the saddest way to die - alone, with no-one to mark your passing. Cheryl Menzies-Runciman from LifeRites explains that this should not be the case, since they are an organisation that can provide trained celebrants to remain with the dying and 'bear witness' as they pass from this world to the next. "LifeRites also offers a pre-funeral plan where the client can plan their own funeral with a celebrant ready for when the times comes. Copies may be lodged with the client's will and also a copy is held at LifeRites central office so that arrangements can be quickly put into place when needed."

A pagan priest of their own Tradition can arrange for the dying person's wishes to be carried out in the strictest confidence and here we must stress that there are no rules. Everyone is an individual and even in death, different people will have wholly dissimilar needs: it's not a pagan priest's job to be judgemental. A priest of their own faith in attendance maybe all they need to allow themselves to just slip away, drawing comfort from the knowledge that there is someone there to watch over them on a spiritual level.

The same criteria apply in coping with a death watch. The paramount issue when sitting beside someone as they pass over into the next life is to offer kindness and reassurance. A person about to leave is in a vulnerable state, and they will require a peaceful atmosphere and quietness. Here, small considerations can play a large part in helping a person to move over peacefully. Scent, for example, is very evocative and, used wisely, can be of great benefit. If, for example, you were going to talk quietly, taking the person on a pathworking, then scent could play a useful role. Taking Paul McCartney's lead at the death of his wife, Linda, for example. If someone is known to have strong and happy memories of riding a horse, then a small saddle blanket could be placed nearby, or offered to them to hold, to help the visualisation stay clear and strong by using a familiar smell.

It is, however, inappropriate to start lighting incense unless the dying specifically say that they want it and if they are in hospital, this will not be possible anyway. Alternatively, it may be possible to dab a little of their favourite oil on the temples, or even just place a clean handkerchief nearby with some scent on it. This can be greatly appreciated by both the dying and those at the bedside, as some illnesses can cause an extremely unpleasant body odour.

If a portable cassette or CD-player can be sited nearby, some may appreciate some of their favourite pieces of music playing very quietly in the background. If they do not have a particular favourite, then something soothing, playing quietly may be helpful. Care should be taken not to choose anything too heavy and sombre — nor will a sudden clashing of percussion instruments be appreciated! The death bed is defiantly not a place for clanging bells or thumping drums. And on a purely practical note . . . please make certain that all mobile phones are switched off. Now is definitely not the time for *Colonel Bogey* to fire up!

Similarly, there is little point in writing long involved rituals that are intended for the bedside of a dying person and which involve an abundance of people, noises and clanging about. *They* are unlikely to appreciate it and the only people who will feel better for it are the living. This is selfish in the extreme and certainly not the place for any kind of psycho-drama!

> *"What you can really do for a person*
> *who is dying, is to 'die' with him."*
> [Dr K R Eisler]

Weaving the Web

For the established Traditions, one of the last services fellow members can perform for each other is the 'weaving of the web' or 'cutting of the heart strings'. This is a form of *spiritual* euthanasia inasmuch as the *spirit* is helped to break free and move on, with the priest acting as a companion guide on the first leg of its journey. Jon Randall, who belongs to the Gardnerian Tradition and who also acts as a hospital chaplain, describes the process as follows:

"This is a process and journey that has no time constraints – it just takes as long as it does, but there are distinct linear events that should be allowed for within it. The first is the 'cutting of the heart strings', allowing the emotional separation of the dependent ties between them and their loved ones. This may sound uncaring, but it facilitates the passing with less worry for them and their partner/family. It does not remove 'love', conversely it is a supreme sacrifice that strengthens it.

"From hereon in, it is the priest and patient as companions, conversing, using a specific terminology, designed to reassure both patient and any others that may be in the room. A point of note should be that no formal circles of any kind should be cast; they will only act as a barrier, either physically or mentally. If it has been possible, you will both have made a practice of this journey before, or have discussed the shared imagery to facilitate it. However, as with all trips things can change, someone who has seemingly come to terms with their passing may suddenly get 'cold feet' and get very tense, upset or nervous.

"This is something that you should be prepared for, but should not be allowed to upset, or alarm loved ones. A firm, but compassionate manner is a necessity... consider yourself as an authoritative matron ... commanding, but fair. This will reassure both the patient and their family; the one thing that is an assurance for both is your professional manner. Like the child who needs walking to the school gate on their first day, you as a companion can only go so far, you have to stop and watch them as they take those all important steps, to start a whole new experience - yes, they may look back, but assure them that it will be fine, and there will be new companions for them on the other side, just as there were here.

"A couple of final things. First, if the patient is known and loved by you, do your personal 'emotional cleansing' prior to this, or after as appropriate, but not at the point of this final journey. It is not cold to do so, but will help reassure the patient to accept their passing, seeing that you are able to take control and not be over-emotional. Secondly, the greatest honour you can do the dead is to remember them by living."

However a death watch is conducted, peace, quiet and reassurance are all that are needed. Under these circumstances, basic human kindness and sensitivity is the mark of a good pagan priest or priestess, not the ability to be an accomplished stand-up performer. An effective priest/ess should have the experience and the inner resources to be able to handle every situation according to its needs having the knack of being able to speak, quietly and honestly to the patient, without being condescending. From this normal, everyday talk, they should be able to gently ease the dying person into a pathworking, which will take them back to a favourite time in life. Guiding them safely and surely on a journey that will lead them to the ultimate moment of departure smoothly, and almost unnoticeably. This is a true kindness, however long it takes, and however much others may not want them to go.

Hysterical weeping and wailing will only hinder, frighten and confuse the about-to-be-deceased. It will effectively keep dragging them back to a mortal shell that can no longer sustain them. This is cruel and selfish, and here a priest/ess must exercise strength and authority in having these people taken out of earshot. A quiet word of explanation may help them to understand that the soul needs quietness and gentleness to pass over. After all, one would not scream at a baby to hurry up and come out! No one would want a brass band thundering out as they make their entrance into this world. It is new, and it is scary - and it is no different when we die.

Having said all this, consideration should, of course, be shown to relatives of a dying person at all times. And despite the religious beliefs, it is pointless attempting to implement rites designed for an entire group around the bedside, if there are close relatives who would prefer to be simply left alone. Bear in mind that the about-to-be-deceased may never have been able to discuss their beliefs with the family; they may simply not have had time to explain that an unknown priest/ess may be there, which may be the case where a sudden accident has occurred.

Great sensitivity must always be shown, for there is nothing to be gained from using any form of bullying tactics no matter how veiled they are. Sudden death has an unpleasant habit of throwing up difficult situations and this is not the time to be discussing rights and principles. For example, Michael Dunn posed the question: "What about the person you've been having a secret affair with for the last fifteen years?" Cases where a second family comes to light are not uncommon and the priest/ess will need all their political and social wits about them to cope with whatever crops up.

There may be problems if a relative turns up who is fanatical about another faith: here the discussion (or argument) *must* be removed out of earshot of the patient. Though this is neither the time nor the place, not everyone (especially a fanatic) will be compliant or considerate. A competent priest/ess must be able to explain that the important issue is the comfort of the dying, but in a short no nonsense manner, since it is not appropriate to enter into long, theological discussions in some hospital corridor. In the event of an emergency, if a fanatical relative becomes too distraught to reason with, then one of you would have to consider withdrawing. The patient may be dead by the time you sort it out!

At no time should group members ever give the impression that they are trying to muscle any outside relatives or friends away from the bedside. This type of behaviour, however well intentioned, can lead to the type of publicity that implies cults and control. Neither must the pagan priesthood overstep the boundaries of the law or religious propriety, regardless of the pressures put on them to do so, and one area where religious beliefs can collide is in the refusal to grant any form of absolution for the dying.

A spokesperson for the Temple of Khem, a contemporary magical Order based on the ancient Egyptian Mysteries, said that although they catered specifically for those of the Khemetic Tradition, they still considered themselves in the same light as a service padre, in that they would administer to anyone in an emergency.

"After all death doesn't always hang around for the appropriate folk of a particular religious denomination to be present. It would be similar to a Christian priest saying to a dying Jew on the battlefield 'Sorry old son, you'll have to hang on for the rabbi!' It would be uncharitable if not downright cruel not to offer some form of comfort, but it is *not* within our power to grant absolution. The Khemetic belief is that you take total responsibility for your actions in life; after death it's between you and your gods and no one can intercede on your behalf. Some people just want you to say the magical words so they can die with a clear conscience, but this would go against the tenets of our own beliefs.

"That said, nursing and funeral staff always seem surprised that we're so 'normal'," the ToK spokesperson continued. "They half expect us to turn up in fancy dress, sporting a papier-mâché crown or something, rather than wearing just a simple business suit. In fact, it's a policy that no member of the Order is allowed to wear *ritual* robes in public, not even to conduct a funeral. Admittedly there are certain rites which are peculiarly Egyptian in content but discretion is always our watch word, whether we attend the bedside or the graveside."

On a final note:

It is advisable to request that the body be left for a couple of hours before being removed, in order for the departing spirit to 're-condition' itself to its new perspectives. Sometimes the spirit becomes confused and hovers around its body, unsure of what steps to take. If possible, the priest should remain on watch to deal with such happenings and to ensure that the spirit moves on with the minimum of discomfiture.

> *"Men fear death as children fear to go in the dark;*
> *and as the natural fear in children is increased with*
> *tales, so is the other."*
> [Francis Bacon 1561-1626]

The Spirit Having Flown

The old saying that "the dead can't harm you" is perfectly true when people are fit and well, but the fear of whatever is waiting of the other side can cause terror for those who are suddenly confronted by the reality of having a dead body on their hands.

Remember that under no circumstances can a body be moved before a doctor has certified the cause of death. Until then, there can be no formal laying-out or funerary preparation. If members of the family, or friends from a pagan group have volunteered to do this according to the deceased custom or Tradition, then this can be carried out with the co-operation of the funeral director.

Once the doctor has examined the body and written out the Death Certificate, this should be taken in person by the next of kin, to the local Registrar of Births, Deaths & Marriages for the death to be registered, otherwise the funeral cannot go ahead. The Registrar will issue a Certificate for Burial, which must be given to whoever is arranging the funeral and if cremation is preferred, a second independent doctor will need to complete an additional form to certify cause of death, and that no further examination of the body is necessary. If the family is contemplating keeping the body at home until the funeral, it should be mentioned that without the refrigeration facilities of the funeral home, there could be one or two unpleasant surprises waiting just around the corner.

Bodies will begin decomposing after about two days and the acceleration rate varies according to the age of the person and the cause of death. If the family wish to keep the body at home until the funeral, it will need to be kept in the coldest part of the house (no central heating on!) There are stories about bodies being kept at home, with the window open to keep the room cool ... during high summer ... and the flies got in ...

If the deceased has been fitted with a pacemaker, this must be removed as they contain lithium batteries that will explode in a cremator. One blast at Morden crematorium caused extensive damage that cost £5,000 to repair. The funeral director is responsible for the correct preparation of all materials entering the cremator and a mistake of this magnitude could be *very* costly.

With so much involved, it is not surprising that most people prefer to allow a sympathetic funeral director to take over the arrangements.

Chapter Four

Preparation
The Rite of Spring (Stravinky)

> *"It is certain that to most men the preparation for death has*
> *been a greater torment than the suffering of it."*
> [Michel de Montaigne 1533-1592]

Should we find ourselves in the invidious position of having to arrange a funeral for a pagan who has been close to us, or for a family well-known to us, one of the first things we need to take into account is who will conduct the ceremony. If we, ourselves, are not a member of the appropriate priesthood, then we will need to arrange for a celebrant to conduct the ceremony according to their religious rites, although the family may wish to remain in charge of all the preparations.

It is also important to liase with the funeral director and ascertain whether he (or she) will be sympathetic to a departure from any standard order of service, and explain why. Bear in mind that many will be unfamiliar with pagan beliefs and it will help if there is a copy of the service available for them to study well in advance of the funeral proceedings.

This will allay any fears (on *their* part) that the local 'crem' will be turned into the venue for a theatrical performance and thereby damage the funeral company's reputation for the future. It will also enable them to pass on this reassurance to the staff at the crematorium.

The funeral industry arranges nearly 700,000 funerals a year and although having three trade associations, it does remain totally unregulated by law. Nevertheless, a funeral director's understanding and familiarity with what needs to be done and can be a great comfort and support to the deceased's family. Most provide a highly competent service but we shouldn't allow ourselves to be bullied into accepting arrangements that we (or the deceased wouldn't have wanted) just because our requests may deviate from the norm. According to one London funeral director (who is himself a pagan), more and more funeral companies are adopting a more positive approach to pagan funerals, but there will always be the odd dyed-in-the-wool traditionalists, who will consider anything slightly left of High Anglican, to be an abomination.

Having said that, the second question that needs to be asked is whether the mourners will be made up of pagans, or outsiders, or a mixture of both.

"When arranging a funeral, the wishes and sensibilities of the deceased's family must always be taken into account. After all, many of them may not know that the deceased was a pagan, let alone a high-ranking Druid or Wiccan. In that case, discreet enquiries would be made so as not to cause offence or fear in some of the more senior members of the family. If the family agree to a pagan funeral, be it cremation or interment, those handling the arrangements should do so with the utmost care and consideration. It may be that guidance is required for, and from the family, as to what is, and what is not appropriate; should traditional robes be worn by the celebrant, or would a dark suit be more fitting for the occasion? Suggestions for readings, poetry, music, etc., can be made if the family is unsure of what to choose."

['The Pagan Perspective' by Suzanne Ruthven
Funeral Director's Journal.]

Both LifeRites and Traditional Life-rites Celebrants insist on a high level of professionalism, each within their own codes of practice. Both organisations are fully aware that death is a sombre rite of passage and will conduct themselves and the ceremony with integrity and decorum. Charges for their services are on par with other similar organisations, although people are often surprised that the pagan priesthood makes any charges. Since they wouldn't expect an Anglican minister to do the job for nothing, why should a pagan celebrant be any different, especially if they have had no former connection with the deceased.

"I am about to take my last voyage,
a great leap in the dark."
[Thomas Hobbes]

Getting It Right

When a priest/ess is requested to perform a pagan funeral for someone not known to them, they should endeavour to find out as much as they can about the deceased as quickly as possible. They should attempt to clarify how committed the person was to their chosen Path or Tradition. This line of enquiry provides time to sit down and think about the information they have been given, and also try to read between the lines, taking special note of how the deceased conducted their life with regard to other people.

If it is clear that the deceased was less than generous in spirit, or less than honest in their dealings with others, they should not pretend otherwise. While these issues do not need to be aired publicly during the funeral service, the wording should be thought out accordingly. Good points could be stressed, but above all the celebrant should not be coerced into telling a pack of lies simply because those left behind want to hear them.

When conducting a *pagan* funerary rite, it should be remembered that, generally speaking, this ceremony is for the deceased; it is a final way of helping that soul to settle onto the new Path that it has taken. It is something of a juggling act to comfort both the living and the dead, and the fact that a *true* pagan funeral is for the guidance of the deceased's spirit or soul, should be gently explained to the living. They have a habit of forgetting that this day is not for them. Nevertheless it is still necessary to take into account the sensibilities of Great Aunt Maud, who may be offended, or scared witless, at being present at what appears to be a satanic rite taking place on a wet Wednesday afternoon at the local 'crem'.

If, as often happens, the priest or priestess is dealing with a situation where the deceased is of one faith, while the living relatives are of another, then the content of the funeral service must be fully discussed well in advance. The details of the rite should be made clear and easy for them to follow; the terminology adjusted to accommodate people who would not understand certain esoteric references. This is not a time for the priest/ess to stick rigidly to their own opinions of how things should be done. Kindness and consideration must be shown to those who are mourning, while still fulfilling the religious obligations to the journeying spirit.

Should the family's religious differences be insurmountable, it may be more appropriate for the pagan mourners and members of the Tradition to arrange for their own memorial rite to take place at a later time. Sometimes this can be carried out when the ashes are to be scattered or interred. In many cases, families who make the most fuss about the content of the funeral service, are the ones who tend to leave the ashes gathering dust on the undertaker's shelf. If there is to be no formal disposal of the ashes, then they may be only to glad and thankful for someone else to complete the task.

In the instance where the deceased has only recently changed their religion, some 'technical' difficulties could arise in the priest/ess being certain that their spiritual needs are actually being catered for. A compromise may have to be reached, if the deceased has not held their current belief very long, simply because it is difficult to determine whether this would have turned out to be a passing fancy or not.

It is up to the experience of the presiding priest or priestess to make an informed decision about this and if they personally feel that the type of service being requested is a travesty of their own faith, then their right to refuse to conduct the ceremony must be respected.

This type of decision and any attendant responsibilities are a very good display of why, especially in certain closed Orders, young people are not sent hurtling through three quick degrees of initiation. A young person simply does not have the *life experience*, to be able to deal with these important spiritual matters, however well intentioned they may be ... and there's more to conducting a funeral than looking good in black!

Chapter Five

Practical Issues
Not A Soul But Ourselves (Marsh)

> *"Human life most nearly resembles iron.*
> *When you use it, it wears out.*
> *When you don't, rust consumes it."*
> [Cato 234-149BCE]

As we have already discussed, what we normally refer to today as funerary rites are predominantly about what to do with the body. We are left with the empty shell of someone we loved and cared about in life and we will wish to dispose of their remains in the most fitting way possible.   Since more and more people are becoming more aware of the more eco-friendly methods of 'burial', it is now unlikely that anyone will even raise an eyebrow if we opt for a green or natural slant for the funeral. What we do need to be aware of, are the options that are available to us:

Burial
For those of a true pagan belief, the prospect of being interred in a municipal cemetery would almost be akin to a second death, unless, of course, there were family reasons for them wanting the burial to take place in the communal plot.   Unfortunately, there are now so many restrictions placed on upon the type of gravestones and memorials we can have, that posterity will never again

be blessed with such national treasures such as Highgate and Kensal Green, and so much of the fun has been removed in preventing us from leaving instructions for some really large and impressive tomb stone to be erected in our memory!

This is why a large number of pagans are opting for 'green' or woodland burials instead. There are now numerous natural and woodland burial sites in Britain run by a variety of organisations – farmers, local authorities, wildlife charities and private trusts or individuals. This means that after burial in a biodegradable coffin, the ground is allowed to settle and a young tree is planted. Eventually a whole tract of woodland will have been created, providing a habitat for wildlife – and a record kept of all the grave locations.

Natural Pagan Burials

"When a very dear friend of ours died, my husband and I had our first opportunity to witness a truly 'green' burial. Although his family were traditional Christians, Tom had been a Druid. He had followed his Path in quiet but devout solitude for most of his life and his funeral took place at a nearby green burial site - and it was from there that the idea of us making natural coffins was conceived. The core of our work is to make and supply traditional hand-woven hurdles from sustainable British woodlands, using hazel, willow and Norfolk reeds and following Tom's funeral, I toyed with the idea of producing both human and pet caskets for natural burial.

"It wasn't until I began studying the history and practices of burial along the way, that I saw how intriguing and relevant the concept was to us now. Making coffins of willow follows a long line of tradition and sentiment. Willow is sacred to Hecate, Circe, Hera, Persephone, all dark aspects of the goddess; to all deities of the Underworld and, in particular, the goddess in her crone aspect – the *Cailleach*, or Old Veiled One. Druidic sacrifices were made at full moon in willow baskets, and funerary flints were made in a willow shape. It could not be more apt in its use as a funerary herb.

"Ancient burial mounds situated near water were often lined with willow, perhaps to keep them from being damaged by water, but probably because of the association with Underworld deities. For a safe journey in another life, it was customary to plant a willow tree during one's lifetime, so that it would continue to flourish long after the planter was dead. It is a tree of death and rebirth. Even the handles of the coffin took on new meaning: some believe that hemp was the *nepenthe* of Homer, the magic potion enabling unhappy mortals to forget their grief.

"Critics of green burials are being silenced by a growing number of supporters. Whether they are pagan, environmentally minded, or merely wishing to have more influence in their own death and burial, people want to create something new and vibrant to mark their lives. This idea often manifests in the form of a tree to be planted in memory of the 'lost' one. There are now over 140 green burial grounds belonging to the Association of Nature Reserve Burial Grounds, who aim to unite farmers and local authorities in producing wildlife habitats and forests from green burial sites, where native trees, wild flowers and protected species of wildlife are encouraged.

"Apart from the obvious benefits of tree planting at woodland burial grounds, even large funeral companies like the Co-op and Golden Charter Funerals are contributing to the replanting of native broad-leaved woodlands by providing the Woodland Trust with donations. As a result, over a million oak, ash and beech trees, have been planted by Golden Charter and the Trust, in recent years. Local councils and even the Roman Catholic Church have expressed interest in green burial sites now that traditional churchyards and municipal graveyards are quite literally bursting at the seams.

"Examine the alternatives: A modern coffin can be made on the factory floor in fifteen minutes. It is usually made of MDF covered by a thin wooden or paper veneer sprayed with chemical varnish. Burying MDF coffins *does* have a hazardous effect on the earth, having the potential to polluting the ground for 20 years, while burning MDF (and the un-biodegradable liners and fittings that usually accompany the coffin), emits dioxins that cause cancer. In fact, 12% of all UK atmospheric dioxin comes from crematoria!

"Undertakers preserve bodies with formaldehyde as a matter of course and this chemical (which again is *very* damaging to the earth and watercourses), is pumped at high pressure into the body to replace the blood, despite only having a very short-term effect as a preservative measure. The pollution due to formaldehyde in the watercourse is not hard to imagine. The ancient Egyptians were undoubtedly more knowledgeable, using tansy and other herbs to preserve the dead much more effectively on a long-term basis. More recently, however, some funeral firms are now using the natural antiseptic sandalwood to preserve the bodies of burn victims, and in cases where formaldehyde cannot be used.

"Burials in a woodland setting are far closer to the surface than traditional burials, which means that the body, with its natural willow coffin, decomposes at a much faster rate, with less chance for the human waste to pollute the immediate area. Over 390,000 wooden coffins are burnt in the UK each year during cremation, and obviously the burning of willow caskets or coffins is obviously preferable. Rather than laying waste to trees, it makes sense to bury or burn a crop that is sustainable, as it only takes one year to grow mature 'withies'. Whether pagan, Christian, agnostic (or any religion), people *are* requesting more environmental burials, and also more control over this Last Rite.

[Abigale Maydon of Natural Fencing

First published in the Samhain issue of The Cauldron 2003]

Cremation

According to recent figures, over 70% of the people in England and Wales prefer the idea of cremation and this certainly makes it easier to dispose of a person's ashes, although many pagans, like Abi Maydon, are concerned about the effects of crematoria emissions on the environment. Under recent EU legislation all crematoria have to comply with stringent regulations in order to reduce environmental pollution, although certain pollutants such as mercury and formaldehyde *do* escape, and continue to cause concern. Nevertheless, a large number of pagans still opt for cremation because the 'crem' allows them to conduct some formal rite within a recognised environment.

The manager of Mortlake Crematorium was quoted in *The Guardian* [1997] as saying: "There is so much help we can give people and, yet, I reckon to get only seven calls a year at most. It's such a shame when they only discover afterwards that they could have done things differently; had a bit more choice, or avoided some aspect of the ceremony which they'd rather have done without ... by contacting us first they can discover the range of choice available and then give their own instructions to a funeral director."

One factor that often rules out cremation is the *size* of the deceased. A family took umbrage because their local 'crem' could not cater for their 22-stone relative, despite the fact that she had expressed the wish to be cremated in the same place as her daughter, who had died three months earlier. Unfortunately, the woman's coffin was 33 inches wide and the maximum width that the cremator could accommodate was 28 inches. This meant that the only option was burial some miles away from where the rest of the family had been interred. This is understandably upsetting but, like the exploding pacemakers, it is far from uncommon.

"Writing for *Pharos* magazine [a monthly journal for members of the 'death-care' community], Dr Jenny Hockey cited a complaint made against Hastings Crematorium concerning their alleged attitude towards pagan funeral practices. In this instance, the funeral rites were only allowed to take place after some 'negotiation about the disposal of the ashes' following cremation. Whether the crematorium's objections were to pagan rites *per se*, or whether there were some difficulties with those conducting the ceremony, were not recorded.

"Following an investigation and in fairness to Hastings Crematorium, the problem resulting in the allegation that the crematorium was biased towards Christian rituals, was one that anyone might have overlooked. The pagan officiant who made the allegations refused to accept that Hastings had no facilities for the disposal of pagan ashes because the gardens of remembrance (and adjoining cemetery) were consecrated to receive Christian, Jewish or Muslim remains, but not pagan. This was not an oversight, since the land was consecrated *before* there was a recognised pagan community and, as the manager pointed out, a similar difficulty could arise with the disposal of Hindu ashes if the family made no arrangements to dispose of them. Generally speaking, from the pagan perspective, very few would wish their ashes scattered in municipal gardens of remembrance because this act in itself goes against the whole ethos of pagan belief.

"Such difficulties can arise simply because of a lack of communication and because pagans themselves often *expect* to encounter objections. When it is explained that the smell of incense or scented candles (an integral ingredient of pagan ritual) would intrude on the next funeral service, rather than being told they cannot use it, the majority would accept the directive without further question."

[An extract from 'A Pagan Insight to Funeral Practice' by Suzanne Ruthven, *PHAROS International*]

"I would rather sleep in the southern corner of a little country church-yard, than in the tomb of the Capulets. I should like, however, that my dust should mingle with kindred dust."
Edmund Burke (1729-97)

Coffins and Options
George Harrison was cremated in a cardboard coffin, while Adam Faith chose a willow casket for his last journey and, whatever any unsympathetic funeral director may tell you, these *are* readily available. There are now all different types of 'casket' that will fit the spirit of the moment and the choice is yours.

+ Many people don't like the thought of a cardboard coffin because of appearing parsimonious to friends and family but there is an alternative in the 'Carlisle Coffin'. This is craftsman made, in beautiful wood with antique carrying handles: a 'Compakta' cardboard coffin fits inside. The Carlisle Coffin can be used for viewing the deceased and for any ceremony, and after the cremation service the interior one slides out and the outer shell is used for another funeral. This significantly reduces the cost of a funeral and reduces the pollution caused by plastics and chipboard in standard coffins.

+ The 'Compakta Coffin' is completely biodegradable and, made largely from recycled materials, it produces little pollution when buried or cremated. Available in woodgrain or white, the latter is ideal for those who wish to paint the exterior.

+ The 'Ecology' is fully biodegradable being made from 86% recycled paper. This coffin has an improved shape and wood finish, which makes it less 'box like' compared to the cheaper Compakta coffin.

+ Bamboo and willow coffins are ideal for both burial and cremation, offering an attractive woven effect in natural plant material. Made from natural fibres, they convey the spirit of earthiness and spirituality.

+ Before the 19th century, bodies were buried in shrouds and this traditional form of funerary regalia is still available today, in the form of the famous 'Carlisle Shroud'. The shroud is made from natural fibres and comprises of a piece of high quality cream wool sheet, woven on the loom in the City of Carlisle. The body is laid on a board and the shroud is then folded in around them. Black cotton ropes are used to lift and carry the body and ultimately, to lower the body into the grave. The ropes are then dropped into the grave over the body and not removed. The shroud is not suitable for cremation.

✦ From the point of personal choice, however, the overall winner has to be the papier-mache Eco-pod. This nifty but disposable little number turned out on the catwalk at the funerary trade's exhibition, shimmering in candle light and sporting a metallic gold exterior with a white feather lining ... now that *is* style! Also available with a Celtic cross.

In addition to their natural willow coffins, Abi Maydon at Natural Fencing has also introduced what they call 'memory' or 'celebration' caskets, which can allow for mourners to add their own 'disposable' mementos that they wish to accompany the deceased. An acquaintance of ours placed all her late father's love letters from the war years in her mother's coffin because she felt that no-one else had the right to read them and keeping them would serve no useful purpose. Abi says: "These caskets can be placed at the rear of the church or chapel and those wishing to add their own memories, poems or mementos can place whatever they like inside." This can be especially useful if the pagan aspects of a funeral are to be played down, as the provision of a casket could offer an opportunity for a separate ceremony should the family exclude pagan mourners from the funerary rites.

> *"In spite of all the learned have said,*
> *I still my old opinion keep;*
> *The posture, that we give the dead,*
> *Points out the soul's eternal sleep."*
> Philip Freneau (1752-1832)
> from 'The Indian Burying Ground'

Choice of site

Natural and woodland burials offer a 'return to nature' for those who wish to be buried with trees and among birds, mammals and wild flowers.   The graves are carefully recorded on a plan, with each being numbered and marked so that every one can always be found as the trees grow and dense undergrowth develops. After the burial, the soil is allowed to settle prior to the planting and at the appropriate time of the year a tree will be introduced to help create a new woodland that will provide a living memorial.

Graves are not reserved for specific religions and the dead of different faiths are usually buried in the same area. Traditional funeral rites do not have to be rigidly followed and it is the family's decision whether they hold a religious service, a secular observance ... or have no service at all. For those who have no relatives to care for a traditional grave, a woodland burial allows Nature to care for the site.

Burials should take place in a biodegradable coffin, shroud or other suitable container but it is advisable to discuss your plans with the managing body. Cremated remains can also be buried in a woodland setting and the requirements will apply to caskets used to contain these – which is where the memory casket can come into its own. Some sites do ask that people keep away from visiting individual graves as trampling through the newly developing undergrowth would create trails and destroy wild flowers.

"Up yonder hill, behold how sadly slow
The bier moves winding from the vale below:"
George Crabbe (1754-1832)

Embalming

Having looked at the options for a natural pagan burial, it should now be evident why embalming should be avoided, and there is little support for it in the medical profession. In many cases the process may be routinely carried out as an inclusive part of the funeral 'package' and without express permission.

If you are personally opposed to embalming, it may be advisable to expressly forbid it, especially as some burial schemes, such as woodland burial, will prohibit the use of chemicals.

DIY Funerals

If you are considering a do-it-yourself funeral, the first place to start is with a copy of *The Natural Death Handbook*, published by the Natural Death Centre and gives highly practical advice on the various options available. This will mean taking on the laying-out and storing of the body; completing all the legal paperwork and acquiring the coffin; transportation to the burial site and organising someone to officiate at the interment. It may be possible to use a funeral director for some of the arrangements, although most would be unwilling to only 'undertake' part of the job.

The Good Death Guide also gives a comprehensive step-by-step guide to arranged a 'home organised' funeral and a large number of pagans do prefer this way. They recommend anyone gets in touch with Heaven on Earth, which offers a whole range of funeral services and were awarded the Best Funeral Shop Award in 1997 from the Natural Death Centre on the strength of the importance they place on customer choice. They will give a little assistance if required, or they can take complete charge.

Chapter Six

Funeral Arrangements
Water Out of Sunlight (Tippett)

> *"Funeral pomp is more for the vanity of the living
> than for the honour of the dead."*
> [Duc de la Rochefoucauld 1613-1680]

At the burial site or crematorium each funeral is allotted a time limit. If you are arranging or officiating, try not to over-run, as it shows a lack of respect to others who may be waiting to say farewell to loved ones of their own. There is nothing worse than having to sit in a funeral car waiting for another bereaved family to leave before your service can begin. The time between one ceremony and the next at a crematorium chapel should also allow for any religious trappings from the previous service to be removed – which should have been previously arranged with the management staff.

Newcastle Borough Council found itself in the middle of a religious row when it removed a five-foot high cross from Bradwell Crematorium Chapel to the Chapel of Remembrance because of the increase in non-religious services being held there. The council reported that around 150 non-religious services were held there each year and between 20-30% of people discussing funeral arrangements *had* asked for the cross to be removed or covered. This upset the local Christian factor and the cross was returned to its original site, awaiting further discussions. Bear in mind that a crematorium is a municipal building not a religious one, and if you wish any religious image to be covered or removed during a funeral, your wishes should be respected.   If using a crematorium for the first time, this issue should be sorted out well in advance and not argued about on the day.

Needless to say, it is important to co-ordinate all the arrangements with the crematorium and funeral director but also pay special attention to the following:

> Who from the immediate family or friends is going to do what?
> Will there be music?
> How are the mourners going to be received?
> Are there any special seating arrangements?
> Can everything be fitted in to the time limit?
> What is the ratio of pagans and non-pagans?

Whatever anyone may say, there are no rules about the content of the ceremony and as there are no formal rites, most of what makes up a pagan funeral is a collection of reminiscences, anecdotes and favourite readings.   What we should also take into account is that most funerals are usually conducted from the survivors' point of view: to console the living rather than observing the funeral rites of the 'crossing over' for the deceased.   In fact, it would be completely *in*appropriate to attempt any form of esoteric rite with non-pagans present, since even the most subtle nuances could make people feel uncomfortable or embarrassed.

The time allocation for the actual ceremony at a municipal crematorium is roughly half an hour and unless you've booked a seasoned performer, there should be some time allowed to run through what everyone wants to do or say. Allow time for reflection (i.e. around 2-3 minutes covers the 'Lord's Prayer' in a Christian ceremony) and anything else the family wishes included but it *is* essential to keep a tight control over the proceedings.

Who from the immediate family or friends is going to do what?

It is now becoming more and more usual for the family to have input into the funeral service, rather than relying on the standard 'service' provided by a duty vicar.

There are always favourite poems or eulogies to be read, but try to ensure that those who volunteer will be able to get through the reading without breaking down. Those organising a pagan funeral will need to ensure that there is one person in overall charge of the proceedings, and as *The Good Death Guide* observes, "and it's important that they can remain sufficiently in control to hold the shape of the ceremony together; it may be that those closest to the deceased should be excused this role".

There is no reason why it cannot be a combined effort with others, but it *does* need co-ordination and planning, especially where there is a combination of pagan and non-pagan elements.

Will there be music?

There are few religions and cultures in which music has played no part at all. As Eric J. Sharpe wrote in *Man, Myth & Magic*: "On the surface, there is all the difference in the world between the music of an African tribal ritual, for instance, and Bach's *St Matthew Passion*, but beneath the differences there is the fundamental resemblance that music is being used to help express and heighten the content of ritual action of some kind. Music is part of the universal language of ritual, and without it ritual must always be impoverished."

It is now so common to include music at a funeral that the Co-operative Funeral Service regularly researches the top ten favourite pieces of music at funerals and cremations, and in recent years the whole top ten has been popular music rather than religious. By rule of thumb, mourners should arrive to something haunting and sedate but at the end of the service the mood can be lifted and lightened.

Wherever would we be without Enya?

How are the mourners going to be received?

The smooth running of a funeral can be helped quite considerably by asking a couple of close friends or family members to act as 'ushers', similar to those normally used at weddings. For one recent pagan funeral, the friends of the deceased spent most of the previous day preparing sprigs of rosemary (for remembrance) to be given to each of the mourners upon arrival. Some preferred to take the sprig home; others dropped them into the open grave on top of the willow coffin.

Don't forget that older mourners may be confused by a breach with the familiar and traditional, so a friendly face directing operations will be appreciated. Following one woodland burial, the 90-year old grandmother of the deceased said that it was the most beautiful funeral she'd every attended, and expressed a desire to have her own follow similar lines. She wasn't at all fazed by the discreet pagan overtones of the ceremony and approved of the 'no nonsense' approach and economy of the willow casket.

Are there any special seating arrangements?

Nearly all families have feuds – more often than not, there is a division between first and second families following divorce and remarriage that will require tactful handling. There is also the possibility that the family may wish to make the funeral arrangements without any acknowledgement of the deceased's pagan beliefs and, should this be the case, any pagan mourners should take seats towards the rear of the chapel unless specifically invited to join the family mourners nearer the front.

Can everything be fitted in to the time limit?

A full pagan rite may be conducted at the crematorium providing it takes place within the time-frame allowed for each funeral, alternatively, a ceremony may take place in 'any separate place of worship followed by a brief committal ceremony at the crematorium'. If you are conducting or arranging the funeral, take the time to run through the whole thing several days before, and if the contributions exceed the allotted time, then you have no alternative – cut!

If there are too many people wanting to contribute, then it might be advisable to hold some form of memorial service at some future date, especially for a specifically pagan oriented rite.

What is the ratio of pagans and non-pagans?

If the pagan contingent is drastically out-gunned then it *will* be necessary to bite the bullet and sit through the traditional funeral service arranged by the family. The message here is 'low key' and another instance where it might be preferable to allow the family to mourn in private and hold a pagan memorial service at a later date. This arrangement is becoming more and more popular with those who have a wide circle of friends and acquaintances (i.e. showbiz personalities); it also allows the family to come to terms with their grief.

If the service is to be held at the graveside, consideration should be given to the time of year, and the average age of those attending. If it's February and freezing cold with a biting wind, and three old aunts over eighty are standing there, it is selfish and thoughtless to drag the proceedings out any longer than necessary. Presuming that the deceased had a fondness for them, they will hardly want them to catch their death of cold!

Remember that woodland burials will provide little shelter from bad weather conditions and few will want to stand around for hours listening to a member of the pagan priesthood banging on about the dear departed leaving for the Summerlands, while the rain drips down their collective necks!

"It isn't pleasant
to know that you are under the earth
even if the place is like an Island of the Dead
with a suggestion of Renaissance."
Eugenio Montale (1896-1981)

Should it fall to you to arrange or officiate at a pagan funeral, keep at the forefront of your mind that on the day people will be vulnerable and looking to you to steer them through it all. Never not forget your role on these occasions. It is likely that you will be invited back to the house for some sort of farewell meal afterwards, and pagan funerals are notorious for the abundance of alcohol made available. Do not be tempted to over indulge because you are sure to become undignified, especially if the deceased was close to you; even as the mourners relax, *you* must maintain your position and behave accordingly.

This can be very important, because in the days and weeks to come, relatives and friends may want to talk to you again, and they must always have confidence and trust in you. The funeral is not over when the undertaker goes home. The entire process may take a few weeks to properly unfold and you should be available throughout this time as a source of support if needed.

The watchword will always be: Consideration, common sense and kindness at all times.

"Excellent ritual of oils, of anointing,
office of priests;
everything was paid before these dead put on
the armless dress of their sarcophagi ..."
Bernard Spencer (1909-63)

What happens if pagan mourners are excluded?

There will be cases where this happens and, as we explained in Chapter One, there is little that can be done about it. If the pagan contingent is excluded on the grounds of religious bias then nothing will be achieved by making any form of protest before or during the funeral. The family may look upon the occasion as having had the opportunity to bring a member back into the fold – even if you know the truth to be different.

Again we return to the idea of some kind of private pagan memorial event, which we will discuss further in the next chapter. In the meantime, on the day of the funeral, and at the appointed hour, ensure that one person from the group can light a candle and leave it to burn itself out as a mark of respect ... your time will come.

Chapter Seven

The Funeral
Song Without Words (Mendelssohn)

> *"It is a fact that a man's dying is more the*
> *survivor's affair than his own"*
> [Thomas Mann 1875-1955]

On the day, the mourners will normally gather at the crematorium in the waiting room, or wait close to the entrance of the burial site a few minutes before the appointed time of the funeral service. It is not usual for a ceremony to commence before the reserved time and so it may be advisable to have people in attendance who can keep everyone together and commiserate with those who may need a word or two of comfort. When the principal mourners are ready to proceed, the coffin will be conveyed into the chapel, or to the graveside by the funeral director, unless family bearers are used by request.

The Crematorium:
If you are conducting or arranging the funeral, ensure that you are at the crematorium well in advance. On average the service will be allowed three quarters of an hour in the chapel – a quarter of an hour to get everyone in and seated, and half an hour for the ceremony. The principal mourners will arrive, together with the coffin, which will be placed on the catafalque. At the moment

during the service when the committal of the body takes place, the coffin may be obscured from view by curtains, or withdrawn mechanically from the chapel. At the end of the service the mourners will make their way outside to make way for the next booking.

In *Vigor Mortis*, Kate Berridge paints a forlorn picture of the aftermath of a cremation. "Behind the crematorium a mass of recent floral tributes lie on the concrete. Flower heads wired to make a ball of knitting and a bingo card, the letters 'UM' in white chrysanthemums (the first 'M' had blown over) – these are poignant reminders that death is a final parting ..."

It will be the family's decision whether flowers should be sent, or whether in keeping with the pagan ethos, donations should be made to a suitable charity. Even if the funeral arrangements stipulate 'no flowers', some thought should be given to placing some sort of floral or herbal tribute on the coffin. Even though we are not carrying out the rite for the approval of any onlookers, it does appear parsimonious if there is not a flower or leaf to be seen. A simple spray tied with ribbons is all that is necessary.

Kate Berridge also goes on to make some further extremely pertinent points: "As a death-style, [cremation] also complements the lifestyle of a society where time is at a premium. Fast food and fast funerals are a twentieth-century sadness, signifying the fact we live at a pace that causes us to experience life and death in convenient, formulaic experiences which ultimately fail to satisfy us ... The slow spread of cremation to the point where it has become the dominant form of disposal of the dead in Britain marks the evolution of a sanitised, secular model of death involving an important transfer of responsibility for disposal away from church to local authority. It also represents a system that has tended to subjugate the wishes of the bereaved, who as a matter of course fall in with the tight timetables of bust crematoria."

In contrast, George Bernard Shaw gave his account of his mother's committal to the flames in 1913: "The feet burst miraculously into streaming ribbons of garnet-coloured lovely flame, smokeless and eager like pentecostal tongues, and as the whole coffin passed in it sprang into flame all over, and my mother became that beautiful fire." At this time, Shaw would have been unaware that the emissions resulting from cremation are now being used to promote 'green burial'.

For those of a pagan spirituality, the 'breeze block and bureaucracy' of the modern cremation process may appear too cold, clinic and detached to fit comfortably with their own beliefs, but it doesn't have to be that way ...

The Graveside:

Woodland interments have far less of the 'conveyor belt' mentality and amongst the pagan community there is a growing trend in which mourners take a more active role in the ceremony. At one woodland burial site it was arranged that a series of bearers would carry the natural coffin to its final resting place. For the first few yards, the deceased's oldest friends carried the coffin; then those who had been work colleagues took a turn; with those who had known the man for the shortest period carried him to the graveside.

Providing the items concerned are biodegradable, mourners often like to place items in the grave (or memory chest) such as photographs, pictures, poems, small clay figures, flowers, shells, feathers, sacred earth ... these things will differ from Tradition to Tradition but they are still part of the funerary process and were known to our ancestors as 'grave goods'. Unless the funeral is a private burial, i.e. one taking place on *privately owned* land, there may be certain restrictions on what can be placed in a grave or coffin – although it is highly doubtful whether any management authority would order the exhumation of a corpse just to retrieve a witch's athame!

More importantly, woodland burials also offer the mourners the opportunity to celebrate the personality of the deceased without any unseemly haste or disapproval by mourners from the next 'consignment', who may or may not be sympathetic to pagan expressions of grief. Whatever personal approach is introduced, however, it is still extremely important that the whole affair be very tightly co-ordinated, even though the interment itself should appear relaxed and informal. If everyone is given leave to express themselves as they please, the whole thing could easily get out of hand, and therefore a strict 'programme of events' should be drawn up and agreed with the family prior to the day of the funeral.

Do remember that Britain's weather is unpredictable and if the deceased is to be laid to rest in   the 'corner of some rural field', then you'd best be prepared to don wellies and a mackintosh rather than the natty little black number you'd set aside for the occasion. Provide plenty of large golfing umbrellas – and make sure that the slippery wet ground doesn't cause more than the coffin to disappear into the grave.

The Ceremony:

An article published in *PHAROS International* highlights the need for some formal guidelines with regard to pagan funerals.   Those who frequent cemetery chapels and crematoria will be familiar with the green *Funeral Services* book, which offers a selection of 44 hymns, and the current cemetery and crematorium rites for the Church of England and the Roman Catholic Church. The benefits of having such a publication available enables people to have what they need to at least follow the funeral service they are attending.

There is no such thing generally available for the pagan community *per se*, especially for those of the more established Traditions and so the service will more than likely comprise of a series of suitable prayers and readings.   This means that it will be necessary to either rely on a celebrant/officiant from one of the pagan organisations conducting the order of service, or scripting your own for the occasion. Generally speaking, the order of service runs as follows:

The Celebration: The celebrant/officiant opens the service with words along the lines of "We are here today to mourn or say goodbye to ..." and says a few words about the deceased as provided by the family.

The Eulogy: If the service is held at a crematorium, there will not be time for a number of people to participate and so the most obvious choice is for a long-standing family friend (or member of the deceased's Tradition) to read a suitable piece.

The Committal: We commit a person's body to the ground or to the flames, and here again the 'religious' nature of the prayer will be governed by the wishes of the family. We can hardly call upon Anubis, Odin or Persephone to guide our deceased pagan if the majority of mourners are non-pagan and haven't got a clue who the celebrant/officiant is banging on about.

The Prayer: As the coffin is lowered or disappears behind the curtains, the mourners can be directed to make their own silent prayers, or engage in a moment's reflection/meditation.

The Close: Keeping a strict eye on the clock if the service is held at the 'crem', the celebrant/officiant should close the service according to the wishes of the family, directing the mourners to any 'funeral feast' if this has been arranged.

Ideally, some form of printed 'order of service' should be handed out, together with details of any planned memorial service, especially if the pagan representatives haven't had their chance to make their formal goodbyes according to their tradition.

The Words:

As we have discussed earlier, there are no official prayers or rituals for pagan rites of passage, although many will turn to the poems of Doreen Valiente – or even Alesiter Crowley - for suitable verses to be read out during the service. As we've seen, where possible, a suitable, short reading should be read by a family member or close friend, *a la Four Weddings & a Funeral*, where W. H. Auden's poem 'Funeral Blues' experienced a new-found popularity following the success of the film.

Another suggested piece may be the following by Henry Scot-Holland, especially if the deceased is a partner or parent:

"Death is nothing at all. I have only slipped away into the next room. I am I and you are you. Whatever we were to each other, that we are still. Call me by my old familiar name, speak to me in the easy way which you always used to. Put no differences into your tone; wear no forced solemnity or sorrow. Laugh as we always laughed at the little jokes we enjoyed together. Play, smile, think of me, pray for me. Let my name be the household word that it always was. Let it be spoken without effort, without the ghost of a shadow on it. Life means all that it has ever meant. It is the same as it ever was; there is absolutely unbroken continuity. What is death but a negligible accident? Why should I be out of your mind because I am out of your sight? I am waiting for you, for an interval, somewhere very near, just around the corner. All is well."

Or one of the Christina Georgina Rossetti [1830-1894] poems:

Remember
Remember me when I am gone away,
Gone far away into the silent land;
When you can no more hold me by the hand,
Nor I half turn to go, yet turning stay.
Remember me when no more day by day
You tell me of our future that you plann'd:
Only remember me; you understand
It will be late too counsel then or pray.
Yet if you should forget me for a while
And afterwards remember, do not grieve;
For if the darkness and corruption leave
A vestige of the thoughts that once I had,
Better by far you should forget and smile
Than you should remember and be sad.

or

Song
When I am dead, my dearest,
Sing no sad songs for me;
Plant thou no roses at my head,
Nor shady cypress tree:
Be the green grass above me
With showers and dewdrops wet;
And if thou wilt remember,
And if thou wilt, forget.

I shall not see the shadows,
I shall not feel the rain;
I shall not hear the nightingale
Sing on, as if in pain;
And dreaming through the twilight
That does not rise or set,
Haply I may remember,
And haply may forget

Another highly suitable poem that has become popular in recent years is the Mahkah Native American prayer:

Do not stand at my grave and weep –
I am not there, I do not sleep.
I am a thousand winds that blow;
I am the diamond glint on snow.
I am the sunlight on ripened grain;
I am the gentle autumn's rain.
When you awaken in the morning's hush
I am the swift uplifting rush
Of quiet birds in circled flight
I am the soft star that shines at night.
Do not stand at my grave and cry.
I am not there; I did not die;

On a more dramatic front, we can draw from the funeral rites of Norse mythology and use an extract from Matthew Arnold's epic poem 'Balder Dead':

But through the dark they watched the burning ship
still carried o'er the distant waters on,
Farther and farther like an eye of fire.
And, long, in the far dark, blazed Balder's pile;
But fainter, as the stars rose high, it flared,
The bodies were consumed, ash choked the pile.
And as in a decaying winter fire,
A charr'd log falling, makes a shower of sparks –
So with a shower of sparks fell in,
Reddening the sea around and all was dark.

Every Tradition will have its own genuine literature from which to draw and although it would be inadvisable to launch into the 'Opening of the Mouth Ceremony' from the ancient Egyptian *Book of the Dead*, with a little bit of thought and foresight, it is possible to create a highly personalised funeral service for virtually everyone of any pagan Tradition.

The Interment or Scattering of the Ashes:

Following cremation the remains are removed and any ferrous and non-ferrous metals separated from the ashes and placed in a special container or urn to await dispersal or collection. The remains of an adult weigh between 2 and 4 kg, although the body of an infant may produce relatively little to collect because of the cartilaginous nature of the bone structure.

In all honesty, human remains resemble cat litter and are almost impossible to 'scatter' or 'throw to the four winds', so there must be some sensible form of disposal planned for after the funeral. In their granular form, the ashes need to be distributed over a wide area of ground as exposure to the elements quickly break down the remains; within a few days little trace of them can be observed.

Many pagans of our acquaintance scatter the ashes over the garden at home rather than have the same act carried out in the local 'gardens of remembrance'. Alternatively, arrangements can be made to have them interred at a woodland site.

The ashes are not usually released until several days after the funeral and although there is not usually any pressure placed on the family to remove them, it is not unusual for the deceased to sit on a shelf at the funeral home for months after cremation! This is often the moment when those pagans excluded from the 'family' funeral can step into the breach.

The family cremated another pagan friend privately, but when it came to disposing of the ashes, everyone was uncharacteristically silent on the subject. In the finish the members of her coven collected the ashes and took them to their own sacred site and with due ceremony and full coven rites, took their own farewells in time-honoured fashion.

Memorial Rite

Memorial services are becoming more and more popular, especially among theatrical families, and should pagan friends be excluded from, or unable to pay their respects according to their own Tradition, holding a memorial rite some time after the funeral is a way of laying the soul to rest according to his or her lights. A woodland glade or mountainside is a long way from the 'breeze blocks and bureaucracy' of the crematorium or municipal cemetery, and is the ideal place to cut the spiritual bonds that may hold the deceased soul, earthbound – regardless of Tradition.

Again, it is sensible for someone to take over the arrangements, but by and large it will an informal affair and will reflect the type of ceremony pertinent to the Path or Tradition. If the past is anything to go by, there will be plenty of music and drumming, with a large fire and plenty to eat and drink – for the pagan ethos is founded on the belief that life is but a stepping stone to death and rebirth.

Chapter Eight

The Grieving Process
Between Silence & the World (Fowler)

*"A certain amount of research on Last Dispatches from
the edge of the tomb has been made, but I feel that
there has always been a tendency on the part of the
imminent mourners to tart the script up a bit."*
[Sir William Connor 1909-1967]

The depth of someone's grief at the loss of a close friend, a member of the immediate family, or partner is largely influenced by the method, or cause of their death. Sudden and unexpected death will be felt differently from those who are released from a slow and lingering demise, where death may appear as a happy release for all concerned. As Michael Dunn points out in *The Good Death Guide*, no two people respond to a death in the same way and the nature of our grief will depend on the attachment we had personally to the deceased, and our 'personal resources to make an alternative life' once the grieving process is over.

For the majority of those of true pagan persuasion, death has lost much of its finality insofar as a genuine magical practitioner has the ability to interact with Otherworld and commune with the dead. This does not mean that the pain of loss isn't as great: it merely means that the Witch, or Druid, or Heathen is more conscious of the *narrow* divide between this world and the next. In

Death & the Pagan

fact, many pagans may be equally as conscious of the two obvious differences behind the burial customs of the diverse cultures that now make up our society: one being the affection for the dead and the other, a fear of them. Fear requires burial in a sealed container, such as a coffin placed six feet underground or a funerary urn. Affection keeps the dead close, both on the mundane and the spiritual levels.

It is, however, important to accept that grief is a natural reaction to loss and that a period of adjustment will, for even the most balanced and stoic of folk, be necessary before we can get on with our lives. As Frances Wilks explains in *Intelligent Emotion*, as we go through life, we lose all sorts of things: parents, pets, friends, loved ones and, in the end life itself. "In order to come to terms with these losses we mourn them until we're ready to let them go. Grief is the doorway from one state to another and it is essential for change and development. Grief doesn't feel very comfortable but it's exactly this discomfort that's needed to force us to move on ... The goal of grief is to achieve an integration at a higher level than we were before we lost the thing we mourn."

There are even recognised stages associated with bereavement: shock, numbness, loneliness, anger, disbelief and even guilt but there is also the over-riding sense of unreality. People often feel that they can't do or say anything constructive until after the funeral has taken place and there specific milestones for the mourning process, which will also include bouts of denial, anger, depression, resignation and finally, acceptance.

Even the most rational of people will go through these stages – even the most committed of pagans.

"No one told me that grief felt so like fear.
I am not afraid, but the sensation is like being
afraid. The same fluttering in the stomach,
the same restlessness ..." C S Lewis

Death often brings about a 'crisis of faith', simply because the member of the priesthood (regardless of denomination) supposedly taking care of the spiritual aspect of the funerary process, finds themselves inadequate when it comes to offering an explanation as to why a particular person was 'taken' at that time of their life.

In *Religion Explained*, Pascal Boyer commented that: "The most natural and the most common explanation of religion is this: Religious concepts are *comforting*, they provide some way of coping or coming to terms with the awful prospect of mortality by suggesting something more palatable than the bleak 'ashes to ashes'." But what if the representative of that religion fails to provide adequate *comfort?*

Unintentionally, Boyer managed to explain why those of pagan belief may find it easier to come to terms with death: "The connection between representations of death and representations of supernatural agents is often considered a question of metaphysics, of how people consider their existence in general".

Pagans generally have a different world-view than the Western monotheistic religions, which tend to suggest that death is some sort of punishment that the deceased have brought upon themselves, rather than it being a perfectly natural process of the eternal life-death-rebirth cycle. Boyer cites this simplistic view in anthropological terms, thereby implying that the more metaphysical attitude to death is the province of primitive people lacking in the religious sophistication of Western monotheism.

Perhaps it is also because pagan belief holds that the spirit of the deceased is about to embark on an important journey that they are also very conscious about the importance of 'letting go'. Excessive mourning may prevent the spirit departing by trapping it in a net of grief from which it is unable to extricate itself and, as a result, may remain earthbound for longer than is necessary. Sometimes, however, the spirit may remain in close contact of its own accord, bringing a form of comfort for those left behind for quite a considerable time.

"I was very conscious of my father for a long time after he'd died," said one priestess. "We'd been very close in life and it was almost as if he was 'there' when there were difficult decisions to be made. Then one day he was just no longer there. It was obvious time for him to move on, too."

In *Secret Flowers*, Mary Jones made this very poignant observation following the death of her husband: ..."Something deep inside me, something that makes me feminine, makes me a woman, needed masculinity ... Without this I was formless, nothing ... A part of me, so basic I had never discovered it before, needed masculinity so that I could remould myself against it ... People said: 'I'm so sorry to hear you've lost your husband,' but what no one seemed to realise was that I had lost myself. And that was much more serious."

It is important to recognise that prolonged or excessive mourning *can* cause physical problems. Appetite and sleep patterns may be disturbed; dizziness and confusion may set in if a reliance on anti-depressants gets out of control; there may be palpitations, chest pains, bladder and menstrual irregularities ... all brought on by the stress of bereavement. Of course, the quickest way to relieve stress is to take regular exercise and a daily walk in the fresh air, could quickly bring the body back into line. Others may suffer a total mental/emotional shut down and be totally incapable of thinking or looking out for themselves. Mostly these effects are temporary, but depression – if allowed to grow untreated – can become a lifelong disability.

If we are lucky, we will have friends and family who can help us through the dark days, but another common side-effect of death is that it often makes friends and neighbours shy away. This can, of course be extremely upsetting but their avoidance may simply be caused by embarrassment in not knowing what to say. On the other hand, just as *"passionate grief does not link us with the dead but cuts us off from them"*, prolonged grief will cut us off from the sympathy of friends and family.

"If I should die and leave you
Be not like others, quick undone,
Who keep long vigil by the silent dust and weep.
For my sake turn to life and smile ...

Nerving they heart and trembling hand
To comfort weaker souls than thee
Complete these unfinished tasks of mine
And I perchance may therin comfort thee."
[Thomas Gray]

Lay off the spirits!

In this case we are referring to the psychic rather than the alcoholic variety, because the former can be equally as damaging to those in a vulnerable state. We often encounter those who have turned to the spiritists following the death of a loved one and have found that, long term, they generally do more harm than good. With the increased interest of science in psychic phenomena since the 1970s, there had been a decreasing interest in spiritism ... that was until the mushrooming of the 'mind, body and spirit' movements which have since fuelled the spirit-mediums to such a degree that there are now adult education courses for mediumship!

Basically, spiritism involves:

(1) A belief in the continuity of the personality after death – that is, the person is more or less the same after s/he has given up the physical body, can communicate in words, remembers events and people, is capable of conversation.

(2) The concept that contact with the dead is possible – the dead exist in some dimension not totally separate from our own and can be contacted there, or alternatively, can come into our dimension to contact us.

(3) People (usually known as mediums) with specific psychic gifts which facilitate communication with the dead by a variety of means – automatic writing, going into a trance, direct voice, etc.

[*The Occult Source Book*, Drury/Tillett 1978]

In terms of pagan belief, however, not everyone approves of the spiritist approach to the dead. "The concept is still deeply rooted in the *Blithe Spirit* type of spirit communication," said a priestess of our acquaintance. "It doesn't matter how *long* the person's been dead, the spiritists still believe they've made a contact: that the dead are sitting around in some sort of parallel afterlife just waiting to pop back on request. It never seems to cross their minds that those unseen entities might just be something a bit more malevolent than dear of Uncle Joe who passed over three days after V.E Day! Why anyone who calls themselves a witch or pagan would want to traffic with these people beggars belief. After all, one of the traits of a *genuine* witch is to summon spirits and get them to respond, so why on earth would anyone *need* the services of a medium?"

Whenever a person close to us dies, they *do* take parts of *our* lives with them. It can be the death of a spouse, a parent, a sibling, a 'best' friend or a lover, but whatever the relationship something has gone that can never be retrieved. In other words, our lives are changed forever.

"I dreamt of you again last night. And when I woke up it was as if you had died afresh. Every day I find it harder to bear. For what point is there in life now? ... It is impossible to think that I shall never sit with you again and hear you laugh. That every day for the rest of my life you will be away."

Carrington, *Diaries*, 17 February 1932. [Lytton Strachery died in January 1932, and Carrington killed herself in March of that year.]

Chapter Nine

Remembrance
The Stone Flower (Prokofiev)

> *"To speak the Name of the Dead is to make them live again.*
> *It restoreth the Breathe of Life to him/her who hath vanished."*
> [Ancient Egyptian funerary text]

Jack Goody in *Man, Myth & Magic* summed up the traditionalists' perspective of death: "Only a full burial will ensure proper despatch to the other world; a partial performance may mean that a dead man becomes not a sanctified ancestor but an unsanctified ghost hanging around his earthly dwelling."

This quote again emphasises those significant differences, discussed earlier in Chapter Two, that divide the neo-pagans from those followers of the more established Orders and Traditions. For the neo-pagan, a simple service observing the niceties of the funerary rite will suffice but as far as the revivalist groups are concerned, this would merely be a throw-back to comfort-Christianity, and provide insufficient preparation to send the spirit of a true seeker on his or her way.

For the revivalists, the correct procedure in releasing the spirit and sending it on its final journey, by observing the proper method of despatch, means that they have fulfilled their obligations to the living memory and the honoured dead. The officiating member of the priesthood *takes the responsibility upon themselves* for the first stage of the spirit's journey and, providing the correct observances have been made, the spirit will cross the 'river' with renewed confidence, rather than in fear. Needless to say, this crossing over cannot be carried out in full view of curious onlookers during a public service at the crematorium, because it is an integral part of the Mysteries ... and this is why it is *not possible* for an officiant from a different organisation, Path or Tradition to conduct the ceremony.

Again, we must avoid the assumption that the revivalist Traditions are merely being smug and elitist, simply because their ways seem *too* pagan, or *too* archaic, for our comfort. We may even take exception because we feel there is an unspoken criticism that the preparations *we've* planned are insubstantial, or incomplete. What must be understood is that many of those of the revivalist or initiatory Traditions have some fifty years of commitment under their belt, whereas the vast majority of those detractors on the neo-pagan paths are relatively recent converts.

A demonstration of this contemporary attitude was expressed when one of the Old Craft Orders announced the passing of the last member of the old family, because they felt that her death should not go unnoticed, and to prevent any false claimants cropping up in the future. A bulletin was placed on the Internet and to the Order's surprise, an unsympathetic and rather flippant response was posted by an anonymous 'name' ...

"I'm seeing Maureen Lipman in a pink twinset casting spells so her grandson will get an 'ology! It scares me. Make it stop! ... We're looking at another of these FamTrads who insist that they are not any one of the imposture groups that impersonate them and they are a genuine 'Old Witchcraft coven'. Yada yada yada. I've lost interest now. Anything that starts implying a lineage going back to the 'Ancient Megalithic Cult' tends to have that effect on me ..."

A spokesperson for the Order replied: "This is, unfortunately, fairly typical of the modern attitude to those with genuine Old Craft connections, largely because the detractors resent anything that implies a genuine lineage. It also goes a long way in explaining why many modern pagans fail to appreciate the importance of observing the traditional death rites required by those of the true Old Ways."

"I'll do as much for my truelove
As any young man may;
I'll sit and mourn all at her grave
For a twelvemonth, and a day.

The twelvemonth and a day being up,
The dead began to speak,
'Oh who sits weeping on my grave,
And will not let me sleep?'"
Anon. 'The Unquiet Grave'

Samhain, or All Hallows

All too often, these traditional acts of remembrance are viewed by many of the modern pagan community as being morbid, obsessed with the past, or as 'death cultism', all of which appear to be at odds with the increasingly happy-clappy approach of contemporary Wicca.   The general impression is that today's interpretation of paganism is uncomfortable with the dead – and this is reflected in the national acceptance of the Americanisation of Samhain, or All Hallows, where the observances have metamorphosed into 'party time. There are even pagans who talk of 'celebrating' the Samhain rite.

Evan John Jones in his book, *Witchcraft – A Tradition Renewed*, says: "For the Hallowe'en ritual the order and symbology differ greatly from those of any other rituals of the year ... It is actually the ancient [Celtic] festival of remembering and communicating with the dead ... and the beginning of winter." In the old Julian calendar, the date would fall around Remembrance Day (11th November) when we commemorate the dead of two world wars – *not generally* a time for thanksgiving.

But neither should it be seen as a time to be melancholy because as the ancient Egyptian text reminds us, speaking the name of the dead *does* make them live again, while we honour their memory and remember the happy times. Traditional British Old Craft in particular observes this ritual in time-honoured fashion, as do the Heathens of the old Norse Tradition.

Fiona Walker-Craven commented that if modern pagans were unable to respect the living, then they were unlikely to respect the dead either. "They sneer at those who stick to the Old Ways and yet want to call themselves 'witch' without having the ability to summon the spirits *and they come*. If they can divine with rod, fingers and birds; can claim the right to the omens *and have them*; have the power to call, heal and curse and above all, can tell the maze and cross the Lethe, only *then* they can call themselves witch. For us, the ancestors never cease to be important. They are an integral part of Old Craft: it is from *them* we draw our power and the courage to cross over and walk in Otherworld."

"If I should go before the rest of you
Break not a flower not inscribe a stone
Nor when I'm gone speak in a Sunday voice
But be the usual selves that I have known.
Weep if you must, parting is hell,
But life goes on,
So sing as well."
[Joyce Grenfell: *Joyce: By Herself & her Friends*]

"I bequeath to ..."

In Chapter One we mentioned the disposal of the deceased's personal effects and magical equipment, and this is often an area that can cause problems if not dealt with correctly. To make no bones about it, we are talking about books and items that may be very heavily 'magically charged' and should certainly not be taken into Oxfam for disposal. In one instance, the family got in a firm of house clearance specialists and the entire magical collection of the deceased was shipped off to a junk shop!

In another case, the house had belonged to a couple who died within weeks of each other and the family enlisted the help of the local auctioneers. "I've never seen anything so tragic as these personal items being pawed over for bargains. Magical robes were being sold at £10 each when they should have been burned!" said one witch who attended the sale. "There was so much stuff that the auction went on all day. There were forty or so crystal balls and I managed to liberate a damaged one, simply because I felt sorry for it. As it turned out, it has been a very useful magical tool and well worth the £5 invested in it." A prized library of occult books met a similar fate.

If named as executor for a magical estate, there are a few pointers about what should happen to certain personal items:

➢ A magical knife or athame should be buried with the deceased, or destroyed. It should never be given to someone else unless specific instructions were given for its disposal *prior* to death.

➢ The deceased should be buried or cremated in their favourite robe and the others ritually burned. The cord should also go with them to the grave.

➢ Magical journals and personal spell books should be ritually destroyed unless specific instructions were given for their disposal *prior* to death.

➢ Books are extremely personal items and should be kept by the executor, or given to those who will appreciate them on a *magical* level.

➢ Magical jewellery should be bequeathed to specific individuals. If this is not the case, then it should be put away somewhere safe until a suitable occasion for presentation arises.

➢ Altar and temple equipment, especially the chalice and the pentacle, should be cleansed and dealt with in a similar manner.

> ➢ Other items, including divinatory tools, can be cleansed and given to friends or members of the group who are of similar persuasion.

By bequeathing personal items to those close to us, we are providing others with magical heirlooms that will become treasured possessions to be handed down when their time comes. If a non-pagan expresses the desire to have a particular object, it will be necessary to weigh the consequences in the balance – but whatever you decide, never hand over any item that has not been thoroughly cleansed of its magical properties.

It also means that as time passes and the pain of loss is less acute, the rites of remembrance can take on an almost festive air. When the dead are spoken about it *is* with a light heart and a feeling that while they have made a head-start on their journey, it will not be long before those who have been delayed on the path of Life, will eventually join them.

Chapter Ten

The Soul's Journey
Uninterrupted Rest (Takemitsu)

> *"I am prepared to meet my Maker.*
> *Whether my Maker*
> *is prepared for the great ordeal*
> *of meeting me is another matter."*
> [Winston Churchill 1874-1965]

Whether we like the idea or not, our dead are always with us ... but this does not mean that we are perpetually haunted by the shades of deceased, wrinkly and cantankerous relatives. Neither does it mean that the newly deceased will be kept earth-bound, in a state of limbo, in case they are needed on matters of earthly importance by those left behind. Our 'ancestors' represent our culture, traditions, heritage, lineage and antecedents; they trace the long march of history that our predecessors have taken under the aegis of a particular Tradition or belief, whether it be that of Witch, or Druid, or Heathen.

When those of a particular Tradition pass beyond the veil, their spiritual essence merges with the divine spirit of the Whole, which in turn gives the Tradition the continuing power to endure – even past its own time and place in history. It therefore remains the duty of the priesthood of the modern revivalist groups to ensure that the soul of the newly deceased can successfully 'join' the ancestors and keep adding to the strength of belief, which, in many instances has already endured for thousands of years. *And this is why it is so important for the proper funerary rites to be conducted by an Initiate of the appropriate Mysteries.*

If when living, we cannot acknowledge and respect the ancestors of the Traditions to which we *claim* to belong, then we will contribute nothing to the Whole when we die. As a result, the ceremony with which we, or our family, choose to mark our passing, will play no significant part in the preservation and continuance of our new-found beliefs. Much of this superficial faith is influenced by what is described in *Exploring Spirituality* as the 'ego-centric' society: where the 'gimme-gimme-gimme' culture demands admittance to all and everything ... spirituality on tap ... without experiencing the need to make any firm and honest commitment to the appropriate Tradition. One of the authors gave us this quote:

"Over the past few decades the focus of religion has moved from being of benefit to the group to being the tool of the individual ... transformed into an ego-centric fad. New Age 'mind, body and spirit' psychology has played a large part in this shift through its emphasis on the individualised member of society. Some schools of psychology teach that all the individual needs is within them and, as a result, many of those following such 'experts' have subsequently become divorced from their spiritual heritage ...

"For practitioners of New Age ideologies the thought processes are a little more insidious. Whereas a considerable amount of the 'mind, body and spirit' approach often denies the existence of external deities, the neo-pagan embraces the notion of every deity in existence, irrespective of its background, preference or allegiance ... These attitudes also reflect the changes from a socio-centric to an ego-centric society, whereby the spiritual focus is not seen as a gathering point for a community, but as a convenient pseudo-spiritual watering hole for the individual. In fact, the cult of the individual now demands that the orthodox beliefs are tailored to meet the requirements of the consumer age and, as a result, folk only want to be bothered with the spirituality of the established Traditions when it suits them."

In many instances we see that, rather than the Elders from the established Traditions being respected for their knowledge and experience, they are resented and, more often than not, held up to ridicule, as per the example given in the previous chapter. At risk of being thought flippant ourselves, perhaps this attitude is best summed up by an extract from one of the novels of Simon Raven, which encapsulates the modern pagan view towards Old Craft and the other established Traditions:

"If I can't, you mustn't; and even if I don't want to, you still mustn't, in case, unknown to me, I'm missing out on something. This is not because I want to understand but can't – I don't give a damn about that – but because someone else might understand and take pleasure in the knowledge, and I couldn't possibly allow that."

Pagan Superstition

But before returning to the concept of the 'ancestors', perhaps we should examine the re-introduction of superstition, which now plays an increasingly more important role in modern paganism under the guise of belief. The word superstition has its root in the Latin *superstes*, a word that includes among its meanings that of 'outliving' or surviving. Used in this sense (*Man, Myth & Magic*), superstition became a useful term for the description of religious ideas that had lived on when the religion from which they sprang had died. The surviving superstitions developed the dual purpose of attracting favourable influences, and warding off unfavourable ones, within the framework of a newly developing folklore and the 'true' religion.

In *What You Call Time*, the author outlined the contemporary definition, pointing out that there is a big difference between superstition and the supernatural, which often clouds today's thinking. "Superstition relies on the slavish belief and implicit trust in 'unexplained' forces. It cultivates fear and promotes a reliance on exterior authority, ultimately perpetuating ignorance. Superstition is used by all suppressive forces, cults and religions to paper over the inconsistencies of their beliefs/philosophies, in order to manipulate the thoughts or perceptions of their followers.

"The supernatural is completely different; this is what *genuine* occultism is *really* about. There are forces that impinge upon humans that are supernatural – these forces exist in many forms, creating changes, mysteries and wonders which science has yet to come to terms with. Testing, invoking, challenging, experiencing and gaining skills to control, direct and benefit from these supernatural forces is magic, and it involves a constant task of self-refinement and the development of self-knowledge."

In similar vein, we take note of the observation made by Justice Tappercoom in Christopher Fry's play, *The Lady's Not For Burning*. "Religion has made an honest woman of the supernatural, and we won't have it kicking over the traces again ... Religion has done its best. But some believe that sooner or later science will do the job more thoroughly, and reveal the supernatural as having been the common-law-wife of nature all along. Yet the supernatural, I suspect, resembles nature in that, though you drive it out with a pitchfork, it will always come creeping back."

What we now have emerging within many branches of modern Wicca and paganism is the 'slavish belief and implicit trust' in the power of the Goddess in much the same way as fundamentalist Christians believe in the power of Christ. In other words, the hundreds of contemporary books promulgating goddess worship are effectively papering over the inconsistencies of the feminine-oriented philosophy, which many believe to be the wholesome catharsis for rejected Christian belief. Instead of a male-god icon, they now have a female-goddess image that they believe to be the all loving, all caring *pagan* deity: an unquestioning devotion that will ultimately metamorphose into a whole new collection of pagan 'superstitions'.

The underlying psychology of these emerging superstitions is clearly defined by the rejection of the true Old Ways of the established Traditions in favour of the pick-and-mix 'all come, all welcome' approach to neo-paganism that required no particular application or study. The popular books tell us this is so, and so we believe it ... we *can* be a witch if we *want* ... but without understanding the fundamental changes, mysteries and wonders of witchcraft. The books also show us that it is no longer necessary to test, invoke and challenge by gaining skills in the art of 'self-refinement and the development of self-knowledge'.

Here we find that another fundamental difference between neo-paganism and the established Traditions is the over-riding inability to differentiate between superstitious observance, and gaining the necessary skills to enable the practitioner to control, direct and benefit from supernatural forces. *Again demonstrating why it is so important for proper funerary rites to be conducted by an Initiate of the appropriate Mysteries* when it comes to the question of the soul's journey into the After Life.

Reincarnation

Belief in reincarnation is very old. Several Greek schools of thought subscribed to it, and Roman writers recorded that it was prevalent among the Gauls and Druids. In later times the doctrine was adopted by the Essenes, Pharisees, Karaites and other Jewish and semi-Jewish religious groups. The Neoplatonists and Gnostics also held the theory and it formed part of the Qabalistic theology of medieval Jewry, although it was rejected by some non-mystics as a sectarian belief alien to Jewish thought. Its fundamentals are basic to Hinduism and most schools of Buddhism and today, most people accept the concept of reincarnation in some form, regardless of their 'family' faith.

The ancient Egyptian religion was strongly based on a belief in the after-life, so how does the Temple of Khem view the subject in its modern context? One tutor explained that they have dozens of students who believe they are 'conscious of having lived in Egypt before' although ToK actually warns against paying too much attention to so-called past-life memories. "Like all things related to the psyche, it is very difficult to draw a distinct line between reality and illusion. Much of what we may like to think as being a link to a former incarnation is, in fact, a set of images that have appeared as a result of us plugging in to the universal subconsciousness, or the *Anima Mundi*.

"These experiences can be extremely 'real' and are no less valid because they come from another level of consciousness. They are merely a form of opening up other channels of communication, sometimes with those with whom we may acquire a form of psychic telepathy and not necessarily ourselves in another life-time. Some people are disappointed at the suggestion that they are not products of different incarnations but personally, I think it is much more exciting to be able to 'link' to other times and places, as this suggests that time may not be linear! Past-life regression (as I see it) serves no useful magical or mystical purpose, and only lines the pockets of unscrupulous practitioners."

Reincarnation is about the soul ridding itself of its accumulated and inherited impurities, in the course of a succession of rebirths, as it evolves towards the goal of perfection. As Benjamin Walker observes in *Man, Myth & Magic*, "The soul must cover a wide range of knowledge and suffering in order to mature satisfactorily ... Many people feel that the theory of reincarnation is in keeping with the idea of evolution and human progress and perfectability ..."

In *Exploring Spirituality*, they quote a little gem of Buddhist philosophy which says that 'If you wish to know of your past life, consider your present circumstances; if you wish to know of your future life, consider your present actions'. In other words, when it comes down to the question of karma and reincarnation, it is all about taking responsibility for our own actions at all times. "It follows the usual pattern, that those who are the most magically, mystically or spiritually inept, are the ones who claim the most fanciful previous life memories for themselves," said one of the authors.

There is the added belief that certain *advanced* beings return voluntarily to earth to help humanity. They are known by various names in the Western Mystery Traditions but in Buddhism, such evolved beings are called Bodhisattvas, and it is believed that some of them have reincarnated again and again. So, although we know that on the psychic levels time is irrelevant in relation to spirit, the probability of an ancient 'soul' emerging in the 21ˢᵗ century without any perceivable spiritual advancement, means that it has learned nothing in its 'sojourn in the vaults of eternity'!

Ancestor worship

A soldier placing flowers on the grave of a fallen comrade met a local man carrying a food-offering to his ancestral tomb. Amused by what he saw as a superstitious absurdity, the soldier asked patronisingly when the man's ancestors would emerge from the tomb to enjoy their meal. "When your friend comes out of his grave to smell your flowers," came the reply.

Here we have the perfect analogy for different cultural attitudes towards the dead. In Western Christian society we believe in honouring the dead on given anniversaries of remembrance, but they rarely take up much of our thoughts for the rest of the time and are certainly not thought of in daily terms. This is because Christian doctrine tells us that the dead are being looked after in heaven and are no longer any of our concern, and to be constantly harping on about our 'ancestors' suggests that the Almighty isn't doing His job properly! It also means that we are perfectly content to put our dead on the back burner, so to speak.

In Africa and Latin America, however, the pre-Christian influences were too strong for even the might of the Catholic church to eradicate, and many of the indigenous native beliefs are still celebrated each year under the auspices of the church. In Mexico, for example, they hold an observance at All Souls (31st October) a custom that combines European pre-Christian and Christian practices with traditional Indian beliefs is the offering of sugared skulls to the dead.

In fact, the basis of ancestor worship is a feature found in *all* human societies: the commemoration of the dead. Although it is important to distinguish ancestor worship proper, from the cult of the dead, which implies a belief in an afterlife of some sort. The worship of the ancestors is focussed on a person's *lineal* kin, on 'those who have socially and physically brought him into being' and s/he retains an open line of communication between the living and the dead - but not in the same manner as spiritists would have us believe.   Maintaining contact with the ancestors does not require the efforts of a third party, or outsider, since observances are made as a matter of course on a regular basis, and the ancestors appealed to directly by the living.

The World's Religions confirms that the cult of ancestors ties in with funerary rites, designed to transfer the dead happily to their resting-places, so they are not consigned to the sad status of restless ghosts but remain important members of the society they have left behind.   Reverence for the ancestors is part of the ethic of respect for those who have preceded you in life and here we think of the spirit world, both divine and departed human, as being close or part of, the visible community in which we have our primary being.

Some of us may see the deceased as individuals until such time as they merge into the generality of our group predecessors. Sometimes an ancestor is reborn *in part* in an individual and, as a result, may function as a kind of 'clan guardian' or exhibit certain supernatural powers. Often ancestors from several generations back are look upon as settled and unthreatening, but the more recent may need to be appeased by propitiatory rites so that they may settle. These are the after death rituals that need to be performed to bring the shade of the departed into the community of the ancestors and reinforce the *importance for proper funerary rites to be conducted by an Initiate of the appropriate Mysteries.*

The Mysteries

But what exactly are these 'Mysteries' and why are they so important to the so-called 'established Traditions'?

Firstly, few people realise the amount of dedication and sheer hard work that goes into a formal Initiation, which involves years of personal study and experimentation. Or the blood, sweat and tears that have been poured into the gaining of knowledge, wisdom and understanding of the Universal Mystery of Life.

Secondly, there is a long period of training and preparation, in readiness for shouldering the responsibility of guiding others along the path. This is a complex and often overlooked area, but a true Initiate has to have confidence that they are capable of dealing with any situation as it may arise, and dealing with it correctly on a personal, magical and practical level.

Initiation into any of the Mystery Traditions is recognised as being dangerous and littered with pit-falls, and that is why teachers take the responsibility of ensuring the would-be initiate doesn't go mad or drop dead during the rite! We know from first-hand experience within our own Tradition, of those who have 'lost it' during initiation, and so take every precaution possible to guide and protect prior to, during, and for sometime after the event.

It should be apparent that *genuine* Initiate would ever reveal details of the 'old Mystery Tradition' – even if they could find the words to describe it. Or as Alan Richardson wrote: "The Greater Mysteries can only be understood through experience; they cannot be taught in words ... That is why it is useless searching books for any True Secret. It does not exist."

Nevertheless, Maurice Maeterlinck managed to write in *Death,* an extremely concise view of immortality, which reflects the metaphysical stance of many Adepts of the Mysteries, especially those with a grasp of Qabalistic philosophy:

"Total annihilation is impossible. We are prisoners of an infinity without outlet, wherein nothing perishes, wherein everything is dispersed, but nothing lost. Neither a body nor a thought can drop out of the universe, out of time and space. Not an atom of our flesh, nor a quiver of our nerves, will go where they will cease to be, for there is no place where anything ceases to be. The brightness of a star extinguished millions of years ago still wanders in the ether where our eyes will perhaps behold it this very night, pursuing its endless road. It is the same with all that we see, as it is with all that we do not see."

"To die will be an awfully big adventure."
[Sir James M Barrie]

Appendix

After Death Comes
A guide to preparing the body

After the point of death, there are a number of requirements, both practical and legal, here we shall examine the preparation and laying out of the body, and it's preparation for the casket, shroud or other final vessel.

It is considered that the body should be touched as little as possible in the immediate aftermath of death, some traditions think that the 'soul' hangs around for a while, and takes time for it to detach itself completely from the physical body. If it is possible, or indeed necessary, the eyes should be shut and the mouth closed. Gently bringing the eyelids down, and taping with surgical tape can achieve this if at all required, and angling the head with a pillow can close the mouth. In all, any necessary contact or touching of the body should be performed gently and lightly.

Usually the hospital or similar venue, will want to move the body immediately following death. This is the usual routine, but you can explain the deceased's beliefs, and they are usually quite happy to delay any removal of the body to allow any necessary ritual, reading, or initial preparation. This is also the point where a family vigil would be most appropriate, but many hospitals now have very well appointed 'Viewing Rooms' which are more private and suitable to the situation.

CHECK:

Please remember it is vitally important not to move the body in any way until the doctor has pronounced the patient dead

Keep the atmosphere in the room serene and peaceful, keep the temperature on the cool side, as this slows natural decomposition process a little. Do not open windows in the height of summer, instead use a fan to keep the temperature down. Remove all blankets from the deceased, and replace with a thin sheet. It is usual for rigor mortis to set in from 3 to 8 hours after death, so be sure to plan all rituals and vigils with this in mind, so you can still prepare the body whilst it is still supple and flexible. rigor mortis will break at about 36 hours after death, but you really don't want to have to wait that long to prepare the body.

All dressed up and no place to go ... Practicalities of body preparation

So the family have finished their vigil, and the rites and rituals have been performed, next we need to wash and dress the deceased for their funeral.

There is no set procedure, however it is best if members of the same sex as the deceased carry out the washing of the body, although in the cases of a spouse or small child there would be valid exceptions to the rule (others would be as common sense suggests). Some Traditions may have people that will do this, but it is often the family that performs this task as a final act of intimacy and respect.

The washing should be performed in a quiet, secluded, private place. A table is preferred, but a hard mattress covered with rubber or plastic sheeting will suffice. If either can be tilted or raised at the head end, then this helps with water run-off. You will need plenty of clean water and soap, plus if the deceased's tradition requires it, some aromatic herbs, perfume, oil, or camphor for the final wash.

Washing should be performed in three phases: Cleaning with soap, rinsing away soap residues and finally rinsing with herbs etc. The deceased's clothes should be removed and then cover the body from navel to knees with a cloth, for modesty. Clean the teeth and mouth first, but do not remove dentures, as they will not go back in. Then, with a piece of cloth wrapped around your hand, wash away any impurities. You can also wear latex gloves for this task if you so desire. Following the cleansing process, you should press lightly on the stomach to expel any remnants, then wash the body for a second time. Each successive washing should be accompanied by a change of cloth, soap, and water.

After the final soap and water wash, you should use just water to remove any residues from the soap, and finally, wash with the perfumed water, if desired. When this has been done, dry the body with a clean towel, and cover with a sheet. You can then proceed to the shrouding of the body.

After the washing of the body, it is advisable to take a shower, not only to clean yourself physically, but also spiritually, and mentally. All materials used during the washing of the body should be burned, which a funeral home or hospital should be able to assist you with. If this proves impossible, place it in a double heavy duty rubbish sack, and pour a bottle of disinfectant into it, sealing adequately.

Jon Randall
Pagan Chaplain
Gardnerian Tradition

Recommended Reading

The Dead Good Funerals Book, Sue Gill & John Fox
Exploring Spirituality, Suzanne Ruthven & Aeron
(How To Books)
The Good Death Guide, Michael Dunn (How To Books)
Life-Rites, Aeron Medbh-Mara (Thoth)
The Natural Death Handbook, The Natural Death Centre
The Oxford Book of Death, D J Enright (OUP)
Religion Explained, Pascal Boyer (Heinnemann)
Vigor Mortis, Kate Berridge (Profile)
What You Call Time, Suzanne Ruthven (ignotus)
The World's Religions, Ninian Smart (CUP)

Useful Contacts & Addresses

Organisations:

Hospice Information Service,
St Christopher's Hospice
51-59 Lawrie Park Road
Sydenham, SE26 6DZ
This service provides facts and figures about hospice care in Britain and abroad for both professional and public enquiries. Local information can be obtained from the Citizen's Advice Bureau. There is a sample information pack available.
Email: his@stchris.ftech.co.uk.

The Natural Death Centre
6 Blackstock Mews
London N4 2BT
Tel: 0207 359 8391
Suppliers of *The Natural Death Handbook* and a registered charity that helps friends and family to arrange funerals with or without a funeral director. They can supply details about existing and proposed burial sites, advise on the availability of coffins, etc., and answer any questions about burial in general.

The Association of Nature Reserve Burial Grounds
c/o The Natural Death Centre
20 Heber Road, London NW2 6AA
Tel: 020 8208 2853
Can supply information as to the location and availability of woodland burial sites all over the country. In many cases it may be possible to reserve space for future use.

Carlisle City Council
Bereavement Services Manager
Cemetery Office
Richardson Street
Carlisle CA2 6AL
Tel: 01228 25022
For general information about burial services, coffins and the 'Carlisle' woollen shroud, Carlisle City Council are leaders in developing a sympathetic approach to death and funerals.

Traditional Life-rites Celebrants
P O Box 6462
Coalville
Leicestershire LE67 2ZU
Tel: 01530 224594
Caters for the more traditional aspects of pagan funerary rites and can offer information about the needs and requirements of the more established Traditions.

The LifeRites Group
Gwndwn Mawr
Trelech
Carmarthenshire SA33 6SA
Tel: 01994 484527
E-mail: info@liferites.org
Website: www.liferites.org
Can be called upon to conduct pagan funerals, as well as counseling and hospice visiting.

Coffins & Options:

Natural Fencing
Suppliers of willow coffins and remembrance chests. The
company has won three national environmental awards for its
conservation work and ethos, including the manufacture of its
willow coffins. See front cover picture.
www.naturalfencing.com

The Somerset Willow Company
The Wire Works Estate, Bristol Road,
Bridgwater, Somerset TA6 4AP
Tel: 01278 424003
Web site: www.somersetwillow.co.uk
E-mail: enquiries@somersetwillow.co.uk
Caskets can be ordered by phone with a next day delivery for the
stock designs and colours. Special orders 48 hours.

ARKA
Supply a range of up-market coffins, such as the gold-leaf,
papier-mache 'eco pod' and a Celtic Cross design.
Tel: 01273 746011

Compakta Limited
Tel/Fax: 01455 828642
Suppliers of cardboard coffins.

The Carlisle Shroud
Carlisle City Council
Bereavement Services Manager
Cemetery Office (see opposite page)
Tel: 01228 25022
A quality woollen shroud suitable for burial.

Index

Further titles available at discount prices from The Hemlock Club

See details of our current and forthcoming titles by sending SAE to the address below or log on to our website at www.ignotuspress.com Titles currently include:

13 Moons by Fiona Walker-Craven
Coarse Witchcraft: Craft Working by Rupert & Gabrielle Percy
Coven of the Scales by Bob Clay-Egerton
Coven Working by Carrie West & Philip Wright
The Egyptian Book of Days by Mélusine Draco
The Egyptian Book of Nights by Mélusine Draco
High Rise Witch by Fiona Walker-Craven
The Hollow Tree by Mélusine Draco
The Inner Guide to Egypt
          by Alan Richardson & Billie Walker John
Liber Ægyptius by Mélusine Draco
Malleus Satani—The Hammer of Satan by Suzanne Ruthven
The Odd Life & Inner Work of W G Gray
          by Alan Richardson & Marcus Claridge
Rites of Shadow by E A St George
Root & Branch: British Magical Tree Lore
          by Paul Harriss & Mélusine Draco
Sea Witch, Paul Holman
The Setian by Billie Walker-John
The Thelemic Handbook by Mélusine Draco
What You Call Time by Suzanne Ruthven
White Horse: Equine Magical Lore by Rupert Percy
A Witch's Treasury of the Countryside
          by Paul Harriss & Mélusine Draco
A Witch's Treasury for Hearth & Garden by Gabrielle Sidonie

ignotus press is an independent publisher whose authors are all genuine magical practitioners, willing to answers questions on any subjects mentioned in their books.

ignotus press, BCM-Writer, London WC1N 3XX

Death & the Pagan

Alphard